Facing up to the Past

# Facing up

Perspectives on the Commemoration of Slavery from Africa, the Americas and Europe edited by Gert Oostindie

Ian Randle Publishers, Prince Claus Fund Library, 2001

to the Past

First published in Jamaica 2001 by
Ian Randle Publishers
11 Cunningham Avenue
Kingston 6

© 2001, the authors, Prince Claus Fund

ISBN 976-637-055-9 paper

A catalogue record of this book is available from the National Library of Jamaica

All rights reserved. No part of this publication may be reproduced, stored in a retrieval system, or transmitted in any form or by any means electronic, photocopying, recording or otherwise without the prior permission of the author or publisher.

**Prince Claus Fund Library**

# Contents

## Africa

9    Gert Oostindie
Stony Regrets and Pledges for the Future

21    Achille Mbembe
The Subject of the World

29    Ama Ata Aidoo
Of Forts, Castles, and Silences

35    Carl Niehaus
Freedom, Yes! … And Then What?

43    Abdul Sheriff
The Slave Trade and Slavery in the Western Indian Ocean: Significant Contrasts

48    Nigel Worden
The Forgotten Region: Commemorations of Slavery in Mauritius and South Africa

## The Americas

56 Ina Césaire
To Each His Commemoration

58 Richard Price
Monuments and Silent Screamings: A View from Martinique

63 Pedro Pérez Sarduy
In Living Memory: The Commemoration of Slavery in Cuba

70 Lowell Fiet
Puerto Rico, Slavery, Race: Faded Memories, Erased Histories

75 Flávio dos Santos Gomes
The Legacy of Slavery and Social Relations in Brazil

83 Livio Sansone
Remembering Slavery from Nearby: Heritage Brazilian Style

90 Hilary Beckles
Emancipation in the British Caribbean

95 Olu Oguibe
Slavery and the Diaspora Imagination

102 Allison Blakely
Remembering Slavery in the United States

109 Seymour Drescher
Commemorating Slavery and Abolition in the United States of America

## Europe

- 114 Frank Martinus Arion
  Un Beau Geste

- 118 Alex van Stipriaan
  The Long Road to a Monument

- 123 Ruben Gowricharn
  The Creole Janus Face

- 127 Harry Goulbourne
  African Slaves and the Atlantic World

- 133 James Walvin
  Slavery, Truth and Reconciliation

- 138 Ratan Vaswani
  A Respectable Trade

The Contributors  147

Acknowledgements  152

# Gert Oostindie

## Stony Regrets and Pledges for the Future

The horror of the transatlantic slave trade is in the past and the legal enslavement of Africans is no longer one of the many injustices still accommodated by the 'New World'. The African diaspora has moved on and into Europe. Not that long ago a cry went up for monuments to be erected to commemorate this sad episode in history, precisely in the places from which the slave trade's chains of command had issued forth. Monuments! Memorials to injustice, a tangible symbol of atonement, preferably a lofty expression of protest against inhumanity. Forgotten are the contemplative words of Nobel Prize winner Derek Walcott, far from his Caribbean island and eye to eye with the colonial statues of the 'Old World':

> 'We had no such erections above our colonial wharves ...
> We think of the past
> as better forgotten than fixed with stony regret.' [1]

### Fin de Millénaire

In a fin-de-siècle mood – perhaps heightened by the realization that an entire millennium was coming to an end – various Western European countries and the United States have been weighing up their own pasts in recent years. Weighing up, and not infrequently condemning events that had earlier been glorified or glossed over in deliberate omission. The spotlights shifted to the now gaping lacunae, to the shrouded side of a past that had previously been portrayed as glorious, or at least honourable. It was as if the centres of power had suddenly grown a special ear for listening to the deafening silences of the past.

This apparently surprising change was by no means all-embracing and certainly not balanced. In Africa, President Clinton expressed his regrets about America's role in the Atlantic slave trade, and the French and Dutch governments openly repented of slavery in their former colonies, one hundred and fifty years post hoc. Yet the same countries had considerably more difficulty with adopting a similarly resolute stance in relation to, for instance, their involvement in Vietnam, Algeria or Indonesia.

---

[1] Derek Walcott, *Omeros* (London: Faber & Faber 1990), p. 192.

Governments do not enter lightly into admissions of guilt; too many risks lie concealed therein. However much they would have liked to express regret – perhaps in a fin de millénaire spirit, but also oiled by the knowledge that such gestures rarely concern their own deeds, but those of their ancestors for whom they can only accept a metaphorical responsibility – their awareness of the presence of a Pandora's box of risks was never far away. The risks are legion when viewed from the seats of power. An erosion of their authority, which after all is founded in part on history. Precedents will be set and gestures might rapidly mutate into obligations. There will be claims from victims, or people who regard themselves as such, who will not be appeased by words alone. There will be protests from the camp of those who were 'good' in the past, who now see their former actions being condemned as 'wrong', while they themselves have never changed their views, nor have been heard. And the steely derision of intellectuals, who accuse their government leaders of obligatory political correctness.

Why then was it the slave trade and slavery which acquired the status of acknowledged subjects for the West's justifiable self-criticism? The horror of this past is indisputable, as is the West's guilt, and hence the unmistakable hypocrisy of this stage in the history of the Western Christian project. But if horror and hypocrisy had been the only criterion, other episodes in national pasts would also have been in line for such public gestures. It undoubtedly helped that the Atlantic slave trade and slavery are completely over, and that they took place long ago – more than one hundred and fifty years for Great Britain and France, and one hundred and forty years for the United Sates and the Netherlands. At a safe distance and always keeping the argument close at hand that at least 'we' ended it ourselves and, moreover, that Africans were also responsible and that they continued much longer, even up to the present day.

Horror, hypocrisy, in the past, space for reflection: on the face of it a fine combination of arguments. And yet these are neither the only, nor the weightiest of arguments. Of far more direct relevance was the appeal from the descendants of Africans who were once taken to the New World as slaves. Their age-old rage had been ignored for just as long and this could not be allowed to continue at the end of the second millennium. In the United States there was the backdrop of the exasperatingly slow and unbalanced process of emancipation of the black population. The anger about the past now threatened contemporary society; to continue to gloss over this past would have dangerously fuelled this anger. In Western Europe a 'colonization in reverse' has taken place from the Caribbean. Formally this was a voluntary expansion of the African diaspora, which also forced a gesture in response to the impatient cry for the West to take its own 'universal' values seriously. A response to a past which had finally found a home in all metropolises.

And so there came gestures of recognition and reconciliation, gestures which in the first instance were aimed at the current situation of the descendants of slaves who now live in the old 'mother countries'. In the same move, at least in theory, a mirror could also be held up to European society. 'This is also our past and it is paramount that we address it and demonstrate the nation's maturity.' And then there was the morality of it all, which in all shapes and sizes came down to the same thing: 'This history will never be over, it can always be repeated; we must be vigilant.'

### Paradoxes, Tricky Demands and the Right to the Last Word

There are paradoxes galore, even today. Unrelenting globalization which is also already and unavoidably rousing its counterpoints and opposing forces. And these forces at times make short shrift of those Western constructions that rely on a delicate balance between values they would like to see being regarded as universal, and the idiosyncrasies of local cultures, which have to be respected precisely because of their idiosyncrasies. There is confusion about humanitarian ideology. Humanitarianism's emphasis on universal human rights lends a glossy veneer to globalization, but it consistently fails to combat the violation of the same rights. And where intervention is possible and worthwhile, it implies, almost by definition, that the delicate balance between universalism and relativism has to be destroyed.

Seen from this perspective, how comprehensive and redemptive then the acknowledgement of the immorality of the Atlantic slave trade and slavery. In truth almost all the speakers in this debate belong to the Western cultural sphere and borrow their arguments from Western ideas on freedom and history. 'The slave trade and slavery contravene human freedom, which is every person's right.' Ergo, these are – in the words of the French parliament – crimes against humanity. It was the same countries who had traded in slaves and used slave labour, either in their own countries or in their colonies, who shortly after the Second World War delivered the Universal Declaration of Human Rights. Ergo, at that time they did not comply with their current norms. A mistake that is now being acknowledged. Not rectified, that's not possible, but in this acknowledgment lies some kind of absolution. And an excellent move it is regarded to be in their own circles. It should not therefore come as a surprise that among the descendants of slaves, however much they may now belong to this same cultural sphere, this 'admission of guilt' and the implicit offer of inclusion is met with scorn. It is also at times painful to see how much effort has to be made within a white public to evoke a feeling of solidarity with a black minority. Steven Spielberg's *Amistad*, with its white heroes, black victims and a few African 'noble savages', unintentionally provides a telling demonstration of this. We all get more worked up about what is going on around the corner than about anything happening on the other side of the world, about what happened here today rather than what happened over there long ago. This inevitably confronts a descendant of a traded African with the fact that the whole history of the slave trade and slavery is far removed from the realm of experience of his or her predominantly white society. Far more removed than his or her own realm of experience – and the resultant discrepancy in compassion can only give rise to even more pain.

Yet the Western world's whole hearted acknowledgement of the horrors that occurred in its past is still a significant step, one that was almost unthinkable half a century ago. And as such it is, let's use that word, progress. A step forward which was forced in the first instance by the 'descendants'. A success for an emancipation movement. The question is, what now? This is currently hotly debated. The claims of the descendants range from simply recognition to monuments, from new school books, museums and research centres to the call for restitution for the descendants of slaves, and the next step, already taken by many: the demand for large compensation payments to be made to the African countries from where those condemned to the middle passage and slavery were once abducted. There is even the illusory hope that the age-old ideas on racial superiority and inferiority which developed through slavery, and the perfidious aesthetic appraisals that accompany them, will be suppressed or reversed as if by an act of God. An illusion as emancipation has to be fought for; it cannot be given.

What is experienced by one person as absurdly exaggerated expectations, is regarded by another as the logical conclusion to those first hesitating steps. It is an illusion to expect that a consensus will grow on this subject. The debate itself is already a small monument to a history that was previously pushed as far as possible into some remote corner of memory. The harsh words that are sometimes spoken, and directed at moderate supporters of memorials, can come across as severe, but this is unavoidable. Do not expect a gratitude expressed through complete conformity. The faint shock that appears to be elicited here and there among 'enlightened', administrative circles has just as much an historical pendant as the prickly reactions of the 'descendants'. It recalls the shock and horror of the nineteenth-century abolitionists, many of whom came from the Christian elites, when they discovered that the slaves, even once they had been given their freedom, did not conform with the behavioural norms of the 'friends of slaves'– in relation to work, authority, sex and family life. The negative impact on public relations for the good cause paralysed the abolitionists. The fear came over many of them that the defenders of slavery might well have been right, that offering freedom was like casting pearls before swine – as if freedom could only take one form.

This, of course, does not mean there can be no open debate about what freedom is, about the interpretation of the past, the conclusions that may be drawn from it, and therefore also the question of what form a commemoration of slavery could or should take. In the debate on the latter there is a tendency among some descendants to capitalize on the victimization of their ancestors, to draw unwarranted and spurious parallels with other drama's from history – primarily the persecution of the Jews by Nazi Germany – and the demand for the right to the first and last word on their own, and in this context suddenly superior, because once African, origins. However, these reactions, at times aggrieved by or intolerant to argument, deserve more than simply jeers, silent dismissal or uncritical acceptance. Now that the memory of slavery is finally on the political agenda it deserves serious attention, even where it's a thorny subject. Contemporary Western universalism, which plays such a major role in the debate on hypocrisy and past shortcomings, postulates the freedom of expression as one of the fundamental human rights. This freedom implies a demand for a critical examination of the past in which the black perspective cannot get away with the pretension of superior 'knowledge of experience'.

The participants in this debate also need to bear in mind that their concerns are primarily those of the 'New World' and its diaspora. Much of this debate has past Africa by. Other more urgent priorities dominate there than a debate about the pain of the descendants of the slaves and the guilt of Western nations – and their African accomplices.

*Facing up to the Past:* An Appeal to a 'Dutch' Public

*Facing up to the Past* is to a great extent based upon a Dutch book that was published in 1999, *Het verleden onder ogen. Herdenking van de slavernij.* This book was written and presented in an explicitly political context. It was an appeal to Dutch society to rediscover forgotten, blood-curdling and shameful pages in its history and thereby to make a gesture towards the descendants of Africans who were once taken as slaves to the Dutch colonies in 'the West', a large number of whose descendants now live in the Netherlands. The tone of most of the contributions to this book was explicitly aimed at convincing a partially sceptical Dutch reading public which was largely ignorant of this history.

My introduction was a short and partial review of the preceding history: early Dutch participation in the Atlantic slave trade and slavery in the Americas; its hypocritical ideological justification; its late abolition of slavery, forced by the British rather than volunteered. In the category of modern countries that the Netherlands dearly considered itself to belong to, it showed itself to be a backward nation. A shameful part of the nation's history which had to be rediscovered. Finally we reached the point where the subject of a monument to commemorate slavery was on the political agenda. This occurred largely because this past came back to the 'mother country' in the most literal of ways through mass immigration from the former Caribbean slave colonies. The presence of these immigrants, I wrote, served as a living reminder of the colonial period and slavery – for those who wanted to see it. However, until recently, there were few who did. This led to increased irritation and frustration in Surinamese and Antillean circles about Dutch ignorance and denial. These emotions became translated into a devoted struggle for recognition which finally fell on receptive ears and led to concrete promises from the government.

But this was not as yet a broad debate, I warned. And even if the government had finally spoken, it was nothing to be proud of. Once again the Netherlands was not at the vanguard. A comparable development had already taken place in other countries where the descendants of slaves had also played a crucial role. In 1998 France had commemorated the abolition of slavery one hundred and fifty years earlier with much emphasis on the subject in parliament and elsewhere. Britain had already held major exhibitions about its involvement in the Atlantic slave trade and slavery. America had done the same, but also added to by Clinton's apologies in Africa. The Netherlands continued to lag behind. Like its involvement in the slave trade and slavery, the reluctant acknowledgement of this past conflicted with the Netherlands' self-image of traditionally being a tolerant and progressive nation.

This is precisely why a clear statement was needed: the Dutch have a responsibility, the slave trade and slavery are part of Dutch history and form links and moral low points in the develop-

2
Gert Oostindie (ed.), *Het verleden onder ogen. Herdenking van de slavernij* (Amsterdam: Arena/Den Haag: Prince Claus Fund 1999).

ment to becoming the modern nation the Netherlands is today. No more, perhaps, but certainly no less. This statement had to be made at the highest level. A sign that the Netherlands is indeed conscious of this past and accepts it as it does the Antilleans and Surinamese in its midst.

Towards a Monument: the Dutch Experience

In this way *Het verleden onder ogen* attempted to contribute to a debate about how the Netherlands could address this past. Words have to be met by actions, a monument, but what kind?

By the time the book was presented, in the summer of 1999, the Dutch government was completely prepared to make a symbolic gesture. The presentation of the book, with much pomp and circumstance, was part of this. The date June 30th was chosen, a date that already has a symbolic status because June 30th and July 1st are the days chosen by many Antilleans and Surinamese to commemorate slavery and emancipation (July 1st, 1863) respectively. Not only was the date symbolic, so too were the venue in The Hague and some of the speakers and guests. The book was presented to an audience of some two hundred and fifty people at the former Dutch parliament building, in active use until a few years ago, but now used for ceremonial occasions. Among the speakers was the Dutch Minister of Metropolitan Policy an Integration Van Boxtel, who expressed his sympathy with the project and its intentions, and who announced that the Dutch government would support, as one practical step, the construction of a monument to commemorate slavery. Among the guests was H.R.H. Prince Claus, the husband of Queen Beatrix of the Netherlands. Creole songs were sung in this former centre of power where slavery had formally been abolished less than one hundred and forty years previously. The whole ceremony had an extraordinarily symbolic, perhaps even a redemptive tone.

Much has happened since then, but far from everything has run smoothly. The Dutch government has since declared that it is prepared to do business with representatives of the descendants of slaves living in the Netherlands. A 'Platform' has been set up and put itself forward as such a group of representatives. On paper it was without a doubt the best qualified to take this position and it was recognized by the government. However, almost immediately the Platform had to contend with legitimacy problems, particularly in Antillean and Surinamese circles. Moreover, a few months later, ministers established their own Recommendation Committee which was regarded by the Platform, not entirely without justification, as a sign that ministers harboured doubts about their first partner.[3]

None of this detracts from the fact that a serious memorial to and reflection on the slave trade and slavery now enjoys broad support. Concrete results are visible. A competition has been held to invite designs for a physical monument, to be built in 2002. Amsterdam City Council has selected a park in the centre of the city for this national monument. And there is much more. There will be a 'dynamic monument' which will combine commemoration, education and research facilities. There will be a television series for schools, school books will be revised, a series of exhibitions will be held in major museums and the government has sponsored a web site.[4] In short, the commemoration of slavery has become socially acceptable. One may ridicule this, but it is a remarkably rapid achievement for a movement that didn't exist ten years ago, and for a cause which at that time would still have been met with a complete lack of comprehension, even scorn.

It is almost impossible for there not to be bones of contention, arguments and issues of competence. These revolve in part around questions of principle: Who should have the final say on the design of the monument? Who, when the time comes, will be placed in charge of running and programming the 'dynamic monument'? Should the government play an active part or merely follow and finance? Can and ought there be a 'black' rewriting of history? How much space should be given to an open debate? What comparisons should or may be drawn with other horror stories and the ways in which we deal with them? In part it is also about the banal wrangling and chicanery that usually arise when there is something that needs to be shared. That's only human.

The discussions about the representation of slavery once again confirm that every past, and certainly such a painful past, is open to interpretation, and that it is not unusual for someone's claim on the truth to be linked to his or her own origins. It would have been naive to think otherwise. Consequently, in the Netherlands too there are now hefty discussions about black and white truth, about whether the 'dynamic monument' will be able to or even ought to cast the past in a completely new light compared with the one that 'white' academia has been shining on it for so long. And so on. A healing discussion in fact, though one which sets many on edge. A Pandora's Box after all!, think some to themselves. Doubtlessly so, but not a cause for panic; neither commemoration nor inclusion imply harmony.

---

[3] See Alex van Stipriaan's contribution to this collection, 'The Long Road to a Monument'. To clarify, Van Stipriaan is an advisor to the Platform, I am a member of the Recommendation Committee.

[4] www.slavernijverleden.nl

Stony Regrets and Pledges for the Future 17

On this Collection

With *Het verleden onder ogen* we – the authors and the Prince Claus Fund, which financed the initiative and arranged for the impressive presentation – aimed at a direct intervention in the Dutch debate. Half of the twenty-six contributions originated from the Netherlands and former Dutch Caribbean colonies. For this section, I also invited papers on the commemoration of suffering among Jews and Indonesian colonial migrants in the Netherlands. The first part aimed to strengthen the case for a monument in the Netherlands. The other half also addressed the commemoration of slavery, but focussed on experiences in other parts of the world. With this second part of the book, I hoped to broaden the scope of what had so far been a rather parochial debate emerging in my home country.

The book, such as it was, indeed helped to spark the debate in the Netherlands. *Facing up to the Past* has different and more modest intentions. Without harbouring any pretensions to making a significant impact on the political agendas in the many countries involved, this collection simply aims to contribute to a more general debate on the commemoration of slavery and to add to our understanding of commemoration and 'the perils of victimhood'.[5] In order to redress the original imbalance, which favoured the perspective of the Netherlands and its former colonies, I had to drop most of the original contributions to the first section. I have retained only two texts: Frank Martinus Arion's 'Un Beau Geste' provided an early, seminal impetus to the Dutch debate, while Ruben Gowricharn's 'The Creole Janus Face' provides a rare critical reflection on the whole enterprise.

Of the 'international' part of *Het verleden onder ogen*, I retained almost all contributions unaltered, apart from some minor updating. This section offers a wide range of perspectives from the Americas, and to a lesser degree Africa and Europe. Several fresh contributions have been added to the present English edition. There is no point in summarizing the twenty-odd papers here present. Suffice it to say that there is a wide and at times competing array of arguments and observations: analyses of how slavery is commemorated or continues to be erased from public memory in particular places; pleas for public action versus criticism of the triviality of official gestures in this field; personal evocations; analyses of the ways artists and educational institutions come to terms with slavery; meditations on truth in historical analysis; and the

5
Ian Buruma, 'The Joys and Perils of Victimhood', *New York Review of Books*, April 8, 1999.

exploitation of victimhood. The decision to divide the book into three 'continental' sections seemed the least disputable option. Even so, the book may be read in any order.

*Het verleden onder ogen* was rather provocatively designed with a prominent black border framing the pages – paradoxically, emphasizing the 'blackness' of these pages in history while at the same time unwittingly borrowing a racist equation of black with the negative. This styling has been dropped since it became apparent that many readers misunderstood or did not register the bitter irony intended. The illustrations in the Dutch edition were partly traditional engravings from the period of slavery and partly modern works of art which address slavery and its legacies. For the present book we have opted mainly for modern works of art, again emphasizing that this is not a book of history, but of history's significance to the present and the future. Particular mention should be made of the inclusion of the nine designs for the actual monument in commemoration of slavery to be erected in Amsterdam within the next year or so. The draft designs were submitted and presented at the City Hall in April, 2001 by nine competing artists invited to contend for the definitive assignment. The artists' own commentaries serve as captions to the respective designs.

Back to the *written* contributions to this collection, the memorials the contributors discuss here are not 'stony regrets', to cite Derek Walcott once more. They are intended to be points of reference, incentives for rethinking and perhaps exorcising the past, and above all pledges for the future: 'never again'. This last objective in particular may sound pretentious, absurd even, and so it is. Yet without such absurd hopes of redemption, the past would be even more painful, and reflections on the future more cynical.

Translation Annabel Howland

Africa

# Achille Mbembe

# The Subject of the World

The spectre of slavery has never ceased to haunt African consciousness. But perhaps more than any other historical event it has haunted it in a paradoxical way, on at least two levels. First, in the mode of victimization. The Atlantic slave trade, more than the trans-Saharan slave trade, has served as the chief symbol of black people's suffering in history. This interpretation of history has been pushed so far as to make it almost impossible to articulate a discourse about Africa that does not reflect this paradigm of victimization. Every discourse that tends to deviate from this paradigm is immediately denounced as 'non-authentic' and 'non-African'. However, the event that constitutes the Atlantic slave trade – and this is the paradox – has been essentially *forgotten* by Africans. Very few Africans accord it any foundational character whatever. Worse still, neither the Atlantic slave trade nor the Arab slave trade, not to mention indigenous forms of servitude, have provided the basis for an African philosophy of life and history or a way of reorganizing the social bond and participating in the world.

### Canonical Meanings

In contrast to the Atlantic slave trade, colonization and apartheid have been conceived in relation to history, politics and culture. Often, they have been used to mask slavery as such, which remains the great unspoken subject. A certain kind of interpretation has tried to assign canonical meanings to colonization and apartheid. Three such meanings are particularly worthy of mention. First, separation from self. This separation is supposed to have led to a loss of familiarity with the self to the point that the subject, having become estranged from itself, has been relegated to an alienated, lifeless kind of identity. Thus, instead of the being-with-oneself (another name for tradition) that it is supposed always to have experienced, it would be constituted in an alterity in which the self no longer recognizes itself: the spectacle of dismemberment.[1] Second, the idea of disappropriation.[2] This process is supposed to involve, on one hand, juridico-economic procedures that have led to material expropriation and dispossession, and on

---

[1] Whether this is called 'alienation' or 'deracination', Francophone criticism has provided the best conceptualization of this 'exit from self'. See in particular A. Césaire, *Discours sur le colonialisme* (Paris: Présence africaine 1950). F. Fanon, *Peau noire, masques blancs* (Paris: Seuil 1952). C. Hamidou Kane, *L'aventure ambiguë* (Paris: Julliard 1961). F. Eboussi Boulaga, *La crise du Muntu* (Paris: Présence africaine 1977). *Christianisme sans fétiche. Révélation et domination* (Paris: Présence africaine 1981).

the other, a unique experience of subjection characterized by the falsification of the self by the other, and then a state of maximal exteriority (*estrangement*) and the ontological impoverishment that this is supposed to entail.³ These two acts (material expropriation and violent falsification) are supposed to constitute the main elements of African uniqueness and of the drama that is its corollary. Finally, the idea of degradation (*avilissement*): not only is the condition of slavery supposed to have humiliated, degraded and tormented the African subject, the latter is also supposed to have undergone an experience of social death characterized by a denial of dignity, dispersion and the suffering of exile.⁴

Following the model of Jewish reflection on the phenomena of suffering, contingency and finitude, these three meanings might have served as the point of departure for a philosophical – and especially, a critical – interpretation of the apparent descent toward nothingness Africa has experienced throughout its history. This would also have required recourse to theology, literature, cinema, music, political philosophy and psychoanalysis. But this did not happen.⁵ In fact, the production of the dominant meanings of these events has been colonized by two ideological trends that are instrumentalist and reductionist, and claim to speak 'in the name of' Africa as a whole. The first of these – which likes to present itself as radical and progressive – has based

2
This applies in particular to Anglophone studies in Marxist political economy. These same studies are sometimes based on nationalist and dependentist theses. For example, see W. Rodney, *How Europe Underdeveloped Africa* (Washington DC: Howard University Press 1981), or S. Amin, *Le développement inégal. Essai sur les formations sociales du capitalisme périphérique* (Paris: Editions de Minuit 1973).

3
Regarding falsification and the necessity of 're-establishing historical truth', see for example the works of nationalist historians such as J. Ki-Zerbo, *Histoire de l'Afrique d'hier à demain* (Paris: Hatier 1972) and C.A. Diop, *Antériorité des civilisations nègres* (Paris: Présence africaine 1967).

4
On the problematics of slavery as 'social death', see O. Patterson, *Slavery and Social Death. A Comparative Study* (Cambridge: Harvard University Press 1982). On 'dispersion' seen from the other side of the Atlantic, see P. Gilroy, *The Black Atlantic. Modernity and Double Consciousness* (Cambridge MA: Harvard University Press 1993).

5
Some plans have, of course, been published here and there. See, for example, the special issue of *Diogène* (no. 179, 1997), 'Routes et traces des esclaves'. Nonetheless, in Africa slavery has hardly been mentioned by theology. In contrast, apartheid has been given a sustained biblical interpretation. See, among others, A. Boesak, *Black and Reformed. Apartheid, Liberation and the Calvinist Tradition* (New York: Orbis 1984). D. Tutu, *Hope and Suffering* (Grand Rapids: W.B. Eerdmans 1984). Colonization has also been interpreted biblically; see, for instance, O. Bimwenyi, *Discours théologique négro-africain. Problèmes de fondements* (Paris: Présence africaine 1981). J.M. Éla, *Le cri de l'homme africain* (Paris: L'Harmattan 1980). On the psychiatric aspects of colonization, see the works of F. Fanon, *Les damnés de la terre* (Paris: Maspero 1961), and *Pour la révolution africaine* (Paris: Maspero 1969), as well as F. Vergès's critique, *Monsters and Revolutionaries. Colonial Family Romance and Métissage* (Durham NC: Duke University Press 1999).

itself on categories inspired by Marxism and nationalism in order to develop an imaginary of culture and politics in which the manipulation of the rhetoric of dependency and autonomy, of resistance and emancipation, serves as the sole criterion for defining an authentic African discourse.[6] Rejecting any idea of *similitude*, the second trend developed on the basis of an exaltation of difference and the native condition. It promotes the idea of a unique African cultural identity founded on membership to the black race.

Of these two trends, the first (Marxism-dependentism) is undoubtedly the one that has done most damage to African thinking. It is characterized by a metaphysical view of history in the name of which its supporters reject, from the outset, the idea that the future is unpredictable. They attribute causality to entities that are fictive and completely invisible, but which they nonetheless believe always ultimately determine the subject. According to this view, the history of Africa can be reduced to a series of phenomena of subjection that are interconnected in a seamless continuity. The difficulty the African experiences in representing himself as the subject of a free, completely emancipated will, is supposed to result from this long history of subjugation. Whence a naive and uncritical attitude with regard to so-called struggles for national liberation and social movements, the exaltation of violence as the best way to achieve self-determination, the fetishizing of state power, the disqualification of the model of liberal democracy and the populist dream of a mass society.[7] Another characteristic of this approach is the will to destroy tradition, and the belief that the true identity is the one conferred by the division of labour that generates social classes, the proletariat (or other subaltern social strata) playing the role of the universal class *par excellence.* Finally, there is a fine irresponsibility, an essentially *polemical* relationship to the world.[8]

[6]
This trend became prominent during the last quarter of the century, in a large number of ideological productions emanating from national institutions such as the University of Dar-es-Salaam (Tanzania) in the 1970s, or from continental institutions such as The Council for the Development of Social Science Research in Africa (CODESRIA) and the Third World Forum in Dakar (Senegal), or sub-regional organizations on the model of the Southern Africa Political Economy Series (SAPES) in Harare (Zimbabwe).

[7]
Cf. the remarks on social movements in M. Mamdani, E. Wamba-dia-Wamba (eds), *African Studies in Social Movements and Democracy* (Dakar: CODESRIA 1995), and M. Mamdani (ed.), *Ugandan Studies in Labour* (Dakar: CODESRIA 1997). See also C. Aké, *The Feasibility of Democracy in Africa* (Dakar: CODESRIA 2000).

[8]
One of the most recent examples of this view is M. Mamdani, *Citizen and Subject. Contemporary Africa and the Legacy of Late Colonialism* (Princeton NJ: Princeton University Press 1996).

The second trend – the nativist one – has never been able to move beyond a polemical claim to cultural specificity. On the philosophical level, its contribution to thinking about African identity is purely essentialist in nature. It refers to slavery only in order to brand it as still another proof of what the West has done to Africa.

But beyond the deficiencies of these two dominant trends of thought on the African subject, it is clear that no order can be imposed that would set limits to the meaning that can be given to the archives constituted by slavery, colonization and apartheid. How could it be otherwise? There is, in fact, no assigned attribute to either the thing nor to any event in itself. These events can only be susceptible to several simultaneous interpretations. That is why once their facticity is acknowledged (once it is admitted that they did in fact occur and that they have structured, for Africans, a certain experience of the world and of the self), the work of reference, of giving meaning, and of putting into signs begins.[9] Concerning reference, Heidegger rightly said that it consists above all in *indicating*. In fact, the sign substitutes what it indicates, 'not only in the sense that it replaces it, but also because the sign itself always *is* what it indicates'.[10] And, one might add, *repeated*. Hence the necessity of asking once again the proper philosophical questions raised by slavery – and by colonization and apartheid. There are at least three such questions.

### The Status of Suffering in History

The first question has to do with *the status of suffering in history*. Here a comparison with other historical experiences is helpful. Let us take the case of the holocaust. The Jewish holocaust, slavery and apartheid represent three forms of *originary* suffering. In each case, there is a dispossession of the self by forces that are unnamable, even though they may take different forms. To the orgiastic giddiness represented by the administration of mass death corresponds, as if by echo, the suspension of life between two rifts, so that the subject no longer knows if he is dead or alive. A destructive impulse and a dislocation of the self and of all individuality constitute the Dionysian background of these events, which are separated by time but linked by a common, extreme disregard for life. On the pretext that origin or race are the criteria of all

---

[9] While to a certain extent this work has been carried out in the United States and in the Caribbean, nothing has been done on the other side of the Atlantic in Africa. In the United States, see, among others, the works of Toni Morrison and Alice Walker.

[10] M. Heidegger, *Being and Time*, trans. J. MacQuarrie and E. Robinson (New York: Harper and Rowe 1962); *Sein und Zeit*, 8th ed., p. 82.

value, forces that have something both dreamlike and intoxicated about them seek to appropriate beings, to exploit them, to express themselves through them, with a mixture of pleasure and cruelty, even in the way they are killed. That is one reason why these events testify against life and censure it, as it were. In the case of slavery and apartheid, it is a matter of Africans' *being-in-the-world*, their life and the forms it takes, as well as what enhances or diminishes it. It is also a reminder that these lives can be *killed* and sacrificed under the influence of sovereignties that are difficult to name, and that are not all of external origin. Lives unworthy of being desired in themselves, in fact. Hence the question of how to redeem them, that is, to shield them from the incessant work of the negative.[11]

### The Work of Memory

The second question has to do with the *work of memory*. Can we summon up slavery, colonization and apartheid as a memory, not as a distinction between before and after, or between past and future, but in their genetic power: the impossibility of a world without others that they reveal, the possibility of multiple ancestries that they indicate, and the weight of Africans' own responsibility in the tragedy – not solely of their own making – that is concealed in their history? Here, the comparison between the African and Jewish experiences reveals profound differences. For example, contrary to the memory of the Jewish holocaust, there is, strictly speaking, no African memory of slavery. Or, if there is a memory of slavery, it is characterized by diffraction. More than an imaginary control, in fact, the set of fragments of metaphors used in sparring matches whose goal is to arouse feelings of culpability while avoiding the responsibilities of the past and at the same time pretending to talk about them.[12] At most, slavery is experienced as a wound whose meaning resides in the domain of the psychic unconscious.[13] Where efforts at conscious recall have been made, they have hardly escaped the ambivalence that characterizes similar acts in other historical contexts.[14]
There are two reasons for this. The first is that between the memory of slavery among African

[11] See A. Krog, *Country of My Skull* (Johannesburg: Random House 1998).
[12] This is the case, for example, in debates about 'reparations'.
[13] Cf. R. Shaw, 'The Production of Witchcraft/Witchcraft as Production. Memory, Modernity, and the Slave Trade in Sierra Leone', *American Ethnologist* 24(4), 1997, pp. 856-76.

Americans and continental Africans, there is a shadowy zone that conceals a deep silence: the silence of guilt and the refusal of Africans to face up to the disturbing aspect of the crime that directly involves their own responsibility. For the fate of black slaves in modernity is not solely the result of the Other's tyrannical will and cruelty – even though the latter is a well-established fact. The other primordial signifier is the murder of the brother by the brother, 'the elision of the first syllable of the family name' (Lacan), in short, the divided *polis*. Along the line of events that led to slavery, this is the trail that Africans seek to erase. A significant ablation, in fact, because it makes possible the illusion that the temporalities of servitude and suffering were the same on both sides of the Atlantic. This is not the case. And it is this *distance* that explains why the traumatism, the absence and the loss will never be the same on the two sides of the Atlantic.[15] As a result, the appeal to race as a moral and political foundation for solidarity will always depend, in some way, on a mirage of consciousness so long as continental Africans have not reconsidered the slave trade and other forms of slavery, not only as a catastrophe that befell them, but also as the product of a history that they actively helped shape by the ways in which they treated each other.

The second reason is of another order. In some parts of the New World, the memory of slavery is deliberately repressed by the descendants of African slaves. The tragedy at the origin of the drama that constitutes their existence in the present is constantly denied, and because it is denied, it cannot provide, by itself, any law or foundation. To be sure, this denial is not equivalent to forgetting as such. It is both a refusal to acknowledge one's ancestry and a refusal to remember an act that arouses feelings of shame. Under such conditions, the priority is truly not to regain contact with oneself and with one's origins. It is not a matter of restoring a full and positive relationship to oneself, since this self has been humiliated beyond all bounds. Since the narrative of slavery is condemned to be no more than an elliptical story, a sort of spectre constantly persecutes and haunts the subject and outlines in his unconscious the dead body of a

---

14
See T.A. Singleton, 'The Slave Trade Remembered on the Former Gold and Slave Coasts', *Slavery & Abolition*, vol. 20, no. 1, 1999, pp. 150-69; E. Bruner, 'Tourism in Ghana. The Representation of Slavery and the Return of the Black Diaspora', *American Anthropologist*, vol. 98, no. 2, 1996, pp. 290-304.

15
On the status of these categories in general and their place in Jewish consciousness in particular, see D. LaCapra, 'Trauma, Absence, Loss', *Critical Inquiry*, vol. 25, no. 4, 1999, pp. 696-727.

16
On these questions, cf. D. Maragnes, 'L'identité et le désastre. Origine et fondation', *Portulan*, no. 98 (n.p., n.d.), special issue on 'Mémoire juive, mémoire nègre. Deux figures du destin'.

language that has constantly to be repressed. For in order to exist in the present, it is thought, one has to forget the name of the father in the very act through which one claims to ask the question of origin and affiliation.[16] This is notably the case in the Antilles.

### The Symbolics of Exile

The third question has to do with *the symbolics of exile*, indeed, the metaphor of the death camp as it is used to compare the condition of slavery with the Jewish condition, as well as with the relationships between race and culture in modern consciousness.[17] There is something hasty about this comparison. In fact, the Jewish imagination constantly oscillates between a number of contrasted myths and unresolved but productive tensions: the myth of autochthony, on one hand, and on the other, the reality of a forced displacement, nomadization and wandering; the empirical fact of dislocation on one hand, and on the other, the expectation of the fulfillment of the promise and the hope for a return; in short, a temporality in suspension in which we can discern the double face of the diaspora and Israel, the absence of territory in no way meaning the interruption of Jewish continuity; and, finally, beyond contingency, fragmentation and terror, a Book, the Torah.[18]

The experience of African slaves in the New World testifies to a more or less comparable abundance of identity, even if the ways in which it is expressed are different.[19] Like Jews in the European world, they have to 'narrate' themselves and 'narrate' a world, and to approach this world from a position in which their life, their work and their language are now almost illegible, enveloped as they are in fantasmatic shapes. They have to invent an 'art of existing' amid *despoliation*, even though it is now almost impossible to re-enchant the past and to cast a spell on the present, except perhaps in the syncopated terms of the body that is constantly made to pass from being to appearance, from song to music.[20] That said, blacks' experience of slavery in the New World as well as in other parts of the world has not been interpreted in such a way as to bring out the possibilities of founding a universal right.

[17]
P. Gilroy, 'Between Camps. Race and Culture in Postmodernity. An Inaugural Lecture', *Economy and Society*, vol. 28, no. 2, 1999, pp. 183-97.

[18]
See Y.F. Baer, *Galout. L'imaginaire de l'exil dans le judaïsme* (Paris: Calmann-Lévy 2000).

[19]
See T. Morrison, *Beloved* (London: Picador 1988).

These three questions suffice to show that by resorting to expedients and not taking up directly these central questions of life, its forms, its possibilities, and what denies it, African criticism, dominated by Marxist and nationalist political economy and by the nativist impulse, has from the outset situated the quest for political identity within a purely instrumental and conjunctural temporality. The various theories of pan-Africanism, like the nationalisms that constitute its practical negation, have their origins in this short-cut. When at the height of colonization the possibility of self-government was considered, it was never to arrive at the general question of being and the struggle for life. From the beginning, the central preoccupation was not the struggle for life, but the natives' battle for political power and control over the state apparatus. In fact, everything comes down to this perverse structure: autochthony. In the prose of the autochthon is exhausted the power of risking death, that is, as Hegel suggested, the ability to put an end to the condition of slavery and to emerge as the subject of a world.

Translation Steve Rendall

20
On these issues, cf. P. Gilroy and C. West. See also S. Hall, 'What is this 'black' in black popular culture?', in: G. Dent (ed.), *Black Popular Culture* (Seattle: Bay Press 1992).

Ama Ata Aidoo

## Of Forts, Castles, and Silences

'From when I was little, all I heard in the classroom about the history of Puerto Rico, was how once upon a time, some Spaniards came to the New World, and after some time, they realized they needed people to work on the plantations, so they went to Africa to fetch slaves, and so the Atlantic slave trade was born, then abolitionists came out to say that the slave trade was wrong, so it was abolished, and now, we are all living very happily ever after. Nobody talks about the cruelties, the suffering, the pain: then, or now. It's the silence. The silence.'
Isabella Moreno, student [1993]

'And yet, there is a bigger crime/We have inherited from the clans incorporate/Of which, lest we forget when the time does come/Those forts standing at the door/Of the great ocean shall remind our children/And the sea bears witness.' [1]

I too had heard that silence throughout my life, growing up in Ghana, West Africa: Ghana, where, arguably between the end of the fifteenth and the middle of the nineteenth century, much of the trans-Atlantic slave trading activities took place. I never heard anyone talk about the slave trade at home, although it had been abolished barely one hundred years before I was born. In school, we were taught the British imperial version of what Isabella Moreno learned from the Spanish colonial, and later, US neocolonial version on Puerto Rico. Yet, Ghana not only boasts most of the forts and castles that survived the years, but also played a major role in the slave trade. In his introduction to *Castles & Forts of Ghana*, the Ghanaian archeologist Kwesi J. Anquandah tells us that by the 'mid-17th. Century, the gold trade was giving way to the slave trade' in Ghana, a country that had earlier acquired its name, the Gold Coast, from a perceived abundance of that precious mineral on its shores! Also from Anquandah we learn that in February 1730 Dutch West-Indian Company Director Rademacher wrote to Holland:

'The Gold Coast has now virtually changed into a pure Slave Coast. The great quantity of guns and gunpowder which the Europeans have brought there has given cause to terrible wars among the kings, princes and caboceers of those lands who made their prisoners of war slaves.'[2]

---

1
Ama Ata Aidoo, *Anowa* (Harlow: Longman 1970).

The size of the Atlantic slave trade was enormous. The trade and its related activities had pervaded almost all aspects of African life for the best part of three hundred years. Yet, as soon as the trade was formally abolished, and later abandoned by even its most zealous perpetrators, the people seemed to have moved quickly – and succeeded! – to erase all traces of it from their memories. In a place like Ghana, a massive wall of silence either accidentally descended, or was deliberately constructed to cover those events. The only opening, and even that quite slight, was provided in the years immediately following independence, when Dr. Kwame Nkrumah's policies attracted into the country a number of African American intellectuals and other activists from the Caribbean and around the world. They had come in search of their roots, or to fulfill long-standing dreams to one day visit, or even live in 'the motherland'. Quite accidentally, but also clearly, such activities compelled the locals to begin to deal – albeit uncertainly – with that sorry part of the recent history of Africans and people of African descent.

The fact that the slave trade was never discussed, could have been the result of either the unplanned byproduct of some collective amnesia; itself an outcome of pain and shame, or of a willful conspiracy of silence that is only challenged by the strength and solidity of the forts and castles themselves. I had asserted in an earlier paper[3] that

> 'we Africans seem to have perfected the development and maintenance of collective amnesia about the past: good or bad. To the eponymous Anowa's persistent attempts to find out who had built the massive forts and what they had been planned for, all she got from her grandmother was: "Shut up, child or your mouth will twist up one day with questions. What devil has entered into you, child? It is not good that a child should ask big questions. You frighten me, child. No one talks of these things anymore! All good men and women try to forget. They have forgotten!"'

We suspect that precisely because each generation of adults refused to discuss the forts, they filled the imagination of each generation of children to the point of explosion. There must have

[2] Kwesi J. Anquandah, *Castles & Forts of Ghana* (Paris: Atalante 1999).

[3] 'A Fairly Grey Dawn' (2000). This paper was a contribution to a collection of essays commissioned for the Emergencia book project by the Swedish museum, Bildmuseet (published, in Swedish, autumn 2000).

been at least forty forts and castles built in Ghana during the period of active slave trading. Over the years, one or two sank into the sea, a few decayed from neglect, while the tropics ruined a couple of others with the merciless sun, the relentless rain and the exuberant organic growths.

In the twentieth century, the castles especially were given different functions to perform. Christiansburg, built by the Danes in 1661 and captured by the Portuguese, had the most visible career. When the British 'inherited it in 1850', they converted it into the seat of government and a residence for the colonial Governor. It kept that role for over one hundred and fifty years, except for about a decade, when as head of state, Nkrumah refused to live or work from there. Cape Coast Castle, built by the Swedes in 1653, named Carolusburg, and captured by the English in 1665, served various functions as a seat of government, a prison, a post office and a tourism promotion centre.

Then there was, and always will be, Elmina Castle (*São Jorge da Mina*). Built by the Portuguese in 1482, captured by the Dutch in 1637, who 'ceded' it to the English in 1872, this is the oldest, the strongest and most notorious of them all. Again from the introduction to Anquandah's volume, we learn that

> 'Outside Ghana, as the Elmina establishment chronologically antedated both Vasco da Gama's opening of the sea route to India and Christopher Columbus' voyage to America, it became the model for the new trading posts in Asia, North America, the West Indies.'[4]

Early last century, it served briefly as the maximum security cell that held the king of the Ashantis on his way into exile in the Seychelles. Later, it became a prison for malcontents, dissidents and all manner of anti-British agitators. Then, in 1972, it was included by UNESCO on the World Heritage List!

On one level, UNESCO's move can be seen as a fine international gesture: a recognition of the fact that the world's collective heritage is a mixed bag of both wholesome and ugly things; Elmina Castle definitely belongs to the latter category! On the other hand, the castle's adoption by UNESCO has led to a certain improvement of its image, which some people consider highly suspect. They think a sanitation process is going on which, not necessarily intended, would eventually cover up, or even remove the more sickening, and damning, evidence of its gruesome history.

4
Op. cit. Anquandah.

On a hill facing Elmina Castle, there is a smaller fort, St Jago. Originally named Coenraadsburg, it was built by the Dutch in the 1660s for the exclusive purpose of defending Elmina Castle. It was also ceded to the British in 1872. When we were in school, we were told that the beautiful shrubbery at the back of this fort was where they used to bury all the people executed in the bigger castle by the colonial government.

One of the interesting, but also rather sad debates on the slave trade had taken the form of a blame game. People spent hours arguing over who had been more at fault: the Africans or the Europeans. One pro-African line was that African leaders of the period had simply succumbed to the ferocity of European firepower, disintegrated morally, and had begun to sell their own people to their conquerors. That would very much have been in line with a tendency for human societies to sacrifice their kin to peevish gods, in a bid to achieve some peace, and extend their own survival. If this was true, then it was a miserable and ultimately useless gesture. For after all, if the formal colonization that followed the 1884/85 sharing out of Africa was any different from slavery, it was in name only. Meanwhile, the pro-European line simply insists that if the Africans had not actively pursued the slave trade with raids and internecine wars, there would not have been any trade at all, or at least, not much to speak of. There is some merit to this argument too: especially when we throw in the fact that some of the most vociferous objections to the abolition came from some notable African kings, including those of Ashanti and Dahomey! However, not only do we now know that so many of the wars were instigated, but also that collectively, Europe did exceedingly well out of the slave trade. Below is some evidence straight from the horse's mouth:

> 'When he came to Guinea, England had 165 slave ships plying the route on Africa, and while Dr. [Samuel] Johnson, [no less!] told Boswell, that one could exist [in London] on 6 pounds a year, the slave traders in Liverpool had a yearly income of 1 million pounds, that were later invested in textile factories, iron foundries, coal mines, stone quarries, canals, docks and railroads.'[5]

Another source of serious hairsplitting was whether the slaves were mostly kidnapped by the

---

[5] Thorkild Hansen, *Slavernes' Kyst* (Copenhagen: Gyldendal 1967). English translation by Kari Dako. Soon to be published by Sub-Saharan Publishers, Accra.

# National Monument to Slavery in Suriname

Jozef Klas, *Liberty Kwakoe*, Paramaribo, Suriname, 1963

'The statue of Kwakoe on the corner of Dr. Sophie Redmond Street and Zwartenhovenbrug Street in Paramaribo is more clearly visible. This sculpture was unveiled on 1 July 1963 by the then Prime Minister of Suriname, Johan Adolf Pengel. It was made by the artist Jozef Klas, who died in 1996. The statue depicts a slave breaking his chains and thus winning his freedom. Kwakoe doesn't represent a particular historical figure, but alludes to the day slavery was abolished. This day, 1 July, 1863, fell on a Wednesday. It was common for slaves to name their children after the day they were born, and a boy who was born on a Wednesday was called Kwakoe. Liberty for the slaves was 'born' on Wednesday 1 July, 1863, hence the statue's name.'
[Extract from: *Suralco Magazine* 1997, Volume 21 no. 1 - *Monuments*]

H. Charpentier, *Place du Nègre Marron*, Diamant, Martinique, 1998

'During the past few months the neighbouring town of Diamant has erected not one but two commemorative monuments – the first, like that of countless other communes in the French Antilles, representing the 'Neg' Marron' (the mythical Maroon, who holds such a central place in the Antillean literary imagination), the other the African victims of a nineteenth-century shipwreck just off the coast. Our fishermen friends see both as consummate wastes of taxpayer money. And the realist-style Maroon, they complain, doesn't look sufficiently 'African' (i.e. savage) – indeed, they say, he looks like 'a (modern) Martiniquan' – while, they complain, the symbolic human figures in the shipwreck memorial are carved from white stone rather than black. Besides, they ask, why dwell on slavery, a shameful period long-since gone?' [Extract from: Richard Price, 'Monuments and Silent Screamings: A View from Martinique' in this book]

Khokho René-Corail, *Nèg Mawon, Arbre de la liberté*, Place des Armes, Lamentin, Martinique, fabrication by Alberto Lescay (Cuba), 1998

Narcisse Ranaresson, *Nègre Marron, Trois Ilets*, Martinique, 1998

Mr. Michael Walsh and Mr. Gerville Rene Larsen, A.I.A., *Middle Passage Monument*, brushed aluminum, 17-feet-wide and 12-feet-tall, 1999

Designed by a multi-racial team of seven metal artists on St. Croix in the U.S. Virgin Islands, the on-land monuments will feature a cubism-inspired, 50-foot arch made of stainless steel. The two-part arch symbolizes the need for the past, present, and future to converge in order for cultural identity and pride to be realized. A 100-foot, granite walkway, each foot representing an estimated million African people who perished during the transatlantic slave trade, will be inscribed with the history of Africa and the Diaspora, ancient and modern, hieroglyphics, symbols, significant dates, events, names, and places. [...]The arch was placed on board the young America, a replica of an 18th-century slaving vessel, and taken to its resting place, 427 kilometers off New York's harbor, facing Africa, where it was lowered onto the ocean floor, perhaps never to be seen again. [...] In order to inspire the living, the Homeward Bound Foundation will place six Middle Passage Memorials around the world in the six regions of the world where the transatlantic slave trade occured, namely Africa, the Caribbean, Central America, Europe, North America and South America. On July 3 of each year between the years 2000 and 2005, a Middle Passage Memorial will be placed in one of the designated regions. [Extract from: www.middlepassage.org/monument.htm]

Ottavio di Blasi, *Gorée Memorial Project*, Senegal, production 2004

The Gorée Memorial Project on slavery in Senegal is debated for the last 13 years. The memorial is not yet built. There has been an architectural competition and the design for the memorial of the Italian architect Ottavio di Blasi won. The memorial project is struggling for funds and at the same time is fighting opposition from public opinion. The pro's and contra's vary from the market women up to the president of state. Some people think it is not necessary to remind us of this painful part of our collective history, others think it is too expensive a project. Some think the money should rather be used to build hospitals and schools. There is an international committee consisting of various members of the cultural and political world from Africa and America. The committee tries to develop this project further and to raise funds. US State Secretary Collin Powell (himself an African American) just donated a high amount of money to develop the project further. [Extracts from correspondence with Koyoh Kouoh, co-operator of the Gorée Institute on Gorée Island, Dakar, Senegal, 2001]

## VI  National Monument to Slavery in Cuba

Alberto Lescay, *Revolution Square*, Santiago de Cuba, Cuba, 1998

'Despite this, until recently there had been no monument to commemorate slavery, until the recent totemic sculpture of Alberto Lescay in the hills surrounding El Cobre, near Santiago de Cuba. There have been, in different periods of the twentieth century, sculptures, museums and monuments that have been allegoric, including the many sculptures dedicated to Major General Antonio Maceo y Grajales, the man who symbolizes and synthesizes the rebellion of all Cubans. […] One of the sculptures erected to the memory of the Bronze Titan (as Maceo, a great mulatto warrior and man of great ideals, was also called) is in Cacahual, on the outskirts of Havana, the country's capital. Another is in the park that bears his name on the Havana seafront, where he is riding horseback facing the centre of the island, not north.' [Extract from: Pedro Pérez Sarduy, 'In Living Memory: The Commemoration of Slavery in Cuba', in this book]

Alberto Lescay, *Untitled*, El Cobre, Santiago de Cuba, Cuba

'In the early 1990s, a sculpture of Maceo was unveiled in Revolution Square in his birth city Santiago de Cuba, which was the most allegorical of its time. The work of black Cuban sculptor Alberto Lescay, it represented the most impressive mausoleum to be put up in Cuba since the 1959 Revolution. The warrior figure of Maceo, also on horseback, can be seen from all angles surrounded by 23 huge structures rising to the sky which represent machetes – the feared toolturned-weapon used by Cuban Creoles and freed blacks when they rose up in arms on 10 October 1868.' [Extract from: Pedro Pérez Sarduy, 'In Living Memory: The Commemoration of Slavery in Cuba', in this book]

Nel Simon, *Desenkadena, National Monument of Curaçao-Dutch Antilles*, erected in 1998. Still photograph from the video documentary 'Desenkadena' by Gloria Lowe.

'*Desenkadena* is the title of the national monument, otherwise known as the 'Tula Monument', to commemorate the slave rebellion on Curaçao in August 1795 in which the slaves Tula, Bastiaan Carpata, and many more rebelled against the conditions of slavery on the plantations and demanded their freedom. The slaves walked off the various plantations and resisted capture for almost four months. The Dutch authorities declared an amnesty for those who voluntarily turned themselves in and placed a bounty on the heads of the leaders of the resistance. Tula, Bastiaan Carpata and Pedro Wacao were captured. They were slowly tortured for several days, than beheaded. In order to serve as public examples, their heads were set on spikes sticking out of the ground on the public highway in close proximity to the beach front area in Otrobanda called Rif. 'Desenkadena' was erected in 1998 at the Rif, which is close to the Rif Fort, where it was common practice to throw away the bodies of executed slaves into the sea. Their bodies later washed up further along the shore at that spot where the monument now stands.' [Text: Gloria Lowe]

whites or their agents, or kidnapped by their black kin and then sold to the whites. Some Africans considered all these arguments equally pathetic, downright insensitive and not worthy of serious discourse. In fact, we felt especially embarrassed by this last argument: because we knew that the Europeans could never have entered 'those jungles' and kidnapped people, unaided by locals. And we could also easily guess the skin colour of those local agents, could we not?! Besides, kidnapped, captured in a slave raid, as war booty, or as merchandise peddled by one's own kin, what difference did it make how you ended up in any of those hell holes, chained to other human beings and free only to sit in yours and other peoples' urine and shit?

If you were frail and lucky, you died on the long march from the interior of the country to any of the coastal forts, or from the violence meted out to you by slave traders and their bully men, or from hunger and fatigue, or from a combination of all these unbearable conditions. If you were strong and lucky, you may have managed to swim ashore even after you had been packed into a ship. But after a certain point, luck ceased to be a factor in the equation and your fate was sealed. You perished, alongside ten to twenty million others whose bones lie on the floor of the South Atlantic Sea. Maybe they tried to swim back or maybe they died from thirst, starvation and disease. Death could also have occurred from summary execution during a revolt on board or, after the revolt had failed, repeated rapes, complications from parturition in impossible circumstances or just, plain, heartbreak.

Only the extremely strong and healthy among the slaves survived everything and reached the shores of the Caribbean Sea or the coasts of the Americas. There too, and finally, the meanest – old and new – cruelties that were ever dreamed up by human imagination were waiting to be perpetrated against their bodies, their minds and their spirits, in yet another long and mind-boggling chapter in human history. What happened to the slaves and their progeny on the other side of the Atlantic Ocean seemed to have been so utterly horrific that the slaves quite often wondered whether their owners and tormentors were indeed human. Feeling very tired, assailed by self-doubts, and therefore dejected in the total way in which only an almost righteous man can know despair, Toni Morrison's character Stamp Paid definitely did wonder, one afternoon:

> 'Eighteen seventy-four and whitefolks were still on the loose. Whole towns wiped clean of Negroes; eighty-seven lynchings in one year alone in Kentucky; four colored schools burned

to the ground; grown men whipped like children; children whipped like adults; black women raped by the crew; property taken, necks broken. He smelled skin, skin and hot blood. The skin was one thing, but human blood cooked in a lynch fire was a whole other thing. On the way home, he stopped, short of breath and dizzy. A moment later, his breath left him again. This time he sat down by a fence. Rested, he got to his feet, but before he took a step he turned to look back down the road he was travelling and said, to its frozen mud and the river beyond, "What are these people? You tell me, Jesus. What are they?"'[6]

Meanwhile, back in Africa, it has been obvious that the various uses the forts and castles were later given only served to temporarily divert any observers' attention from their original purpose as slave auction grounds and holding areas for slaves, before their forced transportation into bonded exile. For after all those centuries, and some serious attempts to deodorize (sic), one lasting characteristic of a place like Elmina Castle is the heavy odour of human misery that seems to pervade all its rooms, corridors and courtyards.

6
Toni Morrison, *Beloved* (New York: Plume Contemporary Fiction 1987), p. 180.

Carl Niehaus

# Freedom, Yes! … And Then What?[1]

I will begin with a personal experience from about fifteen years ago: 'It was a grey overcast day and it started raining softly in the late afternoon. I had to stand on the bed and pull myself up against the bars in order to see through the window. There was only a bare concrete courtyard with dingy brick walls and dark stains where the gutters had leaked. From somewhere, a long way off, came the sounds of steel gates and doors slamming shut. Was that all I was to see and hear for the next fifteen years? I tried to control the rebellious turmoil in me, but the words 'sentenced to fifteen years' spoken quietly, almost expressionlessly, by Judge Myburg referred to a shapeless, immeasurable concept. I tried to quantify the implications: almost two thirds of my age … How many days? I tried to calculate mentally, because they had taken my pen. More than five thousand days, laid like the grey bricks, one after the other, row upon row to form a high unscaleable wall …'[2]

    This was how I experienced my first day in prison. No one understands freedom better than a prisoner. In the bitter isolation of that two by three metre cell I came to know the true meaning of freedom. Freedom is not an abstract concept; it is the concrete source and precondition of free will. The person who is not free has no choices and the person who cannot choose is not a person but an animal – or, worse still, a machine. Freedom is never more sharply focused than when it is denied to you, yet it remains the subject of your most ardent longing. In prison, not a day would pass without having the word freedom on our lips countless times. Sometimes it was the dream of escape – unrealistic, often desperate, futile plans to saw through the steel bars and clamber over the high walls. But we talked most often about what freedom would mean for our country. How the strangling yoke of the apartheid regime could be shaken off. How we, once we had won our freedom, could be worthy of it; and how we would respect the price that had been paid for it.

    This applied particularly to the personal sacrifices that had been made. We knew of them because, in spite of every attempt by the prison authorities to keep us isolated, fragments of news still filtered in from outside. We heard about soldiers in armoured vehicles shooting and

---

[1] This speech was delivered in the Netherlands on 5 May 1998. The fifth of May, Liberation Day, is a national holiday in celebration of the ending of the Nazi occupation during the Second World War.

[2] Carl Niehaus, *Om te veg vir hoop* (Cape Town: Human & Rousseau 1993).

killing schoolchildren. Sometimes it was really close to home, like the morning when, apparently by accident (or was it an accident?) a snatch of the radio news was broadcast over the intercom system in my cell and I heard just enough to realize that Vincent Tshabala, a good friend of mine, had been shot dead in front of his parents' house in Alexandra. The impersonal radio voice described him as a 'terrorist'. On a morning like that, when you walked round the inner courtyard, the scrap of blue sky above you was a duller, greyer colour and you could not speak of freedom lightly.

Rolled up like a parchment scroll, in the hollow leg of the iron bed in my cell was the incomplete manuscript of a book written secretly in this very cell by Bram Fischer – one of the most well-known political prisoners in South Africa and one of a handful of *Afrikaners* who genuinely opposed apartheid. Bram, serving a life sentence, died of cancer a few years before I was imprisoned. He had been incarcerated until he drew his last breath and, even then, his body was never returned to his family. He was cremated and his ashes where thrown away somewhere (one hates to think where: possibly on a rubbish dump?). But this man, who had not even been freed from prison after his death, had argued with great evenhandedness and wisdom for a negotiated settlement. Drawing on the Universal Declaration of Human Rights he had lucidly explained the essential rights, over which there could be no compromise. At the same time he had argued that, in the interest of the quality of freedom, there must be a willingness to come to a settlement with those who still kept us imprisoned at the time, and to share the power of government with them in a democratic manner. Like every prisoner, he wrote with a yearning for freedom, but always with the realization of how much self-sacrifice and discipline it would demand. Time after time the phrase recurred, 'When we are freed, we must do things differently ...'

Yes, when we are freed, we must do things differently ... The universal refrain of prisoners through the ages. Five decades earlier, those condemned to death in Auschwitz and Bergen-Belsen said that to each other, as did those who were held in Japanese camps. Evidently it was also on the lips of those who perished in the recent mass murders of Rwanda and Bosnia. The integrity of such prisoners stands above question. Those who speak of freedom should bear in mind that at this moment and perhaps not too far from here, there is a prisoner who pulls himself up against the bars on his window only to stare at the next wall. Freedom: the great ideal. But is it safe in the hands of the people? One hopes indeed that it is safe, but experience proves the contrary. Freedom is no guarantee of disciplined behaviour. Misuse remains the order of the day. Apathy is raising its ugly head all too quickly once more. Guillaume van der Graft writes:

> 'It never stops. There's no end to it. There's always enough Jews and blacks to kill, enough people to betray, one by one, and words enough to justify it all.'[3]

Freedom is not a natural attribute of society. It is an opportunity, a possibility. It demands continuous maintenance. Freedom has to be learned. Centuries of Eastern philosophies have held that up to humanity: freedom is the arduously earned fruit of a long and hard schooling. No, freedom never falls out of the sky. It is prepared in times of bondage.

Therefore Dutch Liberation Day, 5 May, can only be understood in terms of 4 May, Dutch Memorial Day, just as 27 April 1994 (which we now celebrate every year as 'Freedom Day') can only be understood in terms of Sharpeville, 21 March 1960, when unarmed civilians were shot dead for protesting against the pass laws that made black people strangers in their own country. The youth of South Africa can no longer value their new freedoms and educational opportunities if they forget 16 June 1976, when Hector Peterson and hundreds of other schoolchildren were shot dead during protest marches for equal and non-racial education. Thirty four years lay between Sharpeville and the moment when millions of South Africans could vote for the first time. For us the happiness of that sunny day in late April 1994 is still fresh and new. The excitement feels as if it was only yesterday, when I was able to join the kilometres-long line of patiently waiting people who had returned as many as three times to the voting station in the main road of Alexandra township. I can still smell the dust, trod to a fine powder by thousands of feet, mingling with the ubiquitous smoke of open cooking fires. In spite of the fact that they were the smells of poverty and pollution, triumph tingled in my nostrils, along with the burning sensation in my eyes and nose. From that day on, the poorest of the poor, doomed for so long to live in the townships without any voice, had a vote that was worth the same as that of the well-off, privileged white. I remember the tears of joy coursing down the wrinkled cheeks of an old woman as she raised her walking stick above her head – as though she was calling on heaven as a witness – and shuffled out a few dance steps, crying: *Jaanong nka swa ka kagiso, ka gore ke voutile!*

[3]
Guillaume van der Graft, *Verzamelde gedichten* (Baarn 1982).

(Now I can die in peace, I have voted!) The first ripe harvest of our freedom was our new constitution, ratified in parliament on 9 May 1996, after two years of tough and difficult negotiations.

When I look back on the short years of our freedom, it is like a kaleidoscope of vividly colourful events inextricably woven together. Nelson Mandela walking triumphantly out of prison; three years later, Nelson Mandela voting for the first time; less than a month later, thousands of new flags fluttering over President Mandela on the steps of the Union Buildings in Pretoria for his installation as South Africa's first democratically-elected President, and him calling out: 'It must never happen again that one South African should suppress, or exploit, or hurt another.' But how do we prevent that? What protects freedom from evaporating? Or more serious still: What protects her from the evil of being taken for granted?

In South Africa we are lucky that the realization of the violent struggle and sacrifice through which our people won freedom is still vivid and immediate. But even while the ghastly apartheid past is still so visible and tangibly present, there is already a new generation of young people who are no longer certain of what a Pass was, or how the Group Areas Act worked. How much truer this must be for young people in the Netherlands. The Nazi occupation ended decades ago and a century and a half has passed since the writing of your constitution. How do we keep the memory fresh? How do we ensure that new generations do not simply inherit our freedom, without the discipline necessary to preserve and nurture her? Abel Herzberg wrote in *Amor Fati*:

> 'Now, after a few detours, we have returned from Bergen-Belsen and everything is already a while ago. I watch the memories fade, dull patches appear in our memories. It's understandable enough. It isn't pleasant to constantly look back on awful things, and there are also objections to continuously talking about them. It is not true that cruelty only repulses. It also attracts. Cruelty is infectious. How the camps are written about is therefore not unimportant. In this respect it is of great importance that people not only know what happened, but that they also try to understand it.'[4]

In the Netherlands war memories are sometimes discussed as though they concern only trauma

---

[4] Abel Herzberg, *Amor Fati* (Amsterdam: Moussault 1965).

and the impossibility of assimilation. This is very understandable, even in the second and third generation, who still carry the scars of the war and suffer daily pain. Such people deserve respect. Fortunately, in that country, they get it. It is especially important that they are remembered and that their struggle is never disregarded. We in South Africa have huge numbers of people who have been traumatized by the past: by the torture and the deaths, by the lies and the denigration of an obnoxious regime. Their wounds are still raw. We are convinced that we can only help them and respect them if we keep the memory alive, through research and retelling the stories of our freedom struggle and all that led to our new dispensation. In the short term it does indeed give cause for pain and frustration, but in the long run it will bring healing. We do not want to leave the confrontation to a future generation. The work of the Truth and Reconciliation Commission is, by its nature, specially focused on the apartheid regime and the ghastly crimes against humanity which it committed. But it is not concentrated exclusively on this regime; even freedom fighters who violated human rights are called upon to answer for their crimes. There is great cause for hope in the fact that a commission with such a mandate should have been set up by a parliament, many of whose members are veterans of liberation organizations, serving between them a total of more than six hundred years in prison for their beliefs. The possibility of reconciliation is a reality, but respect for and recognition of the victims must always be in the foreground, no matter whom this might inconvenience.

In the Netherlands too, decades later the memories of war still press insistently forward. More than fifteen hundred liberation monuments already erected bear witness to this. But how can they come to terms with these memories? In all honesty, how is history constructed? It is always easier to commemorate your own history of suffering and heroism than to try to digest the part you played and your responsibility for the suffering of others.

It is absolutely right that the deaths of millions of Jews in the Nazi death camps are remembered, but is enough said of the homosexuals and gypsies who were also murdered? What expatriate Dutch men and women endured in Japanese camps in Indonesia during the Second World War was frightful, and should be commemorated with great sympathy and commitment. But when Indonesia comes up for discussion, should not the long years of suffering of Indonesians under Dutch colonization also be taken into account? Our dedication to freedom should be measured by our will to discuss our full past in the formulation of our present choices. When I consider these things the involuntary thought always presents itself: along with the many liberation monuments, is it not high time we erected a monument in memory of slaves, with a proper acknowledgement of guilt?

But memories are not enough. I say this with particular emphasis when I refer to the times we are living in. In a postmodern environment – in which the master narratives have lost their unifying force – we need to reflect on what binds us together in general. To a certain extent the bond is in our history. But we must not forget that history only deals with the experience of a certain section of the population. The Netherlands and South Africa both have plural societies where there is no longer one history of citizen and nation. If we want to treat fairly all who belong in our varied communities, then we need to do much more than simply teach one national history to all children alike.

In my country millions of black children had history lessons which upheld Jan van Riebeeck and the white boer generals as the only people who bequeathed 'civilization' to us. Shaka, Albert Luthuli and Nelson Mandela were represented as savages. Now South African history is being rewritten. And opting for multiformity puts into perspective the unifying function of our history. Are ideology and language then the unifying factors? What applies to history is also true for the great ideologies and dogmas that so long gave our lives direction and coherence. They have all come under question as a result of the developments in our country and the new historiography. The old deadly enemies in South Africa – Calvinism and communism – have both lost their charisma, to put it mildly.

Even language unites fewer people than before. This is more obvious in a country like mine, with its eleven official languages, than it is in a country like the Netherlands.[5] *Poldernederlands and Algemeen Beschaafd Nederlands* are in conflict phonetically, and also play a role in questions of integration and discrimination. As with our history and philosophical systems, the power of language as a unifying force has diminished.

Then how will we protect and strengthen the freedom of our communities? You solemnly commemorate the Second World War. You celebrate liberation from foreign domination, the last of a long history of attacks on your national identity. Even though the liberation is already half a century old, she has lost nothing of her lustre and glory. But you are also celebrating a hundred and fifty years under your constitution which has not lost any of its lustre either. As a

[5] Yet there too, if I understand the Dutch media correctly, language is a divisive issue.

son of a country which has just received a new constitution from the hands of our freedom fighters, I am convinced that two aspects of this are inextricably interwoven: the freedom won through arduous struggle and the proud language of a document that frames the basis for a people's community. For us in South Africa, the constitution is the marker closing our struggle; from now every citizen in my country can call on a law that treats each person with equality. The much older constitution of the Kingdom of the Netherlands, creating a firm and legal foundation for the prosperity and welfare of your people, is an equally proud possession. The constitutional state is the only firm ground on which the discussion for necessary renewal can take place in a time when so much of what was accepted as fixed identity in the past has been reopened by society for discussion. It is the constitutional state which supports our comradeship. In the face of everything that divides us, every difference of opinion about the execution of governmental leadership, all uncertainty about the changing character of society, the constitutional state gives us the freedom of discussion, of difference of opinion and the freedom to test those things that have kept us together hitherto. The foundation of the constitutional state and the symbol of unity of community is the constitution. That is why it is so meaningful that your hereditary royalty swears the oath on the constitution.

The Netherlands and South Africa have the singular privilege in common that we both have Heads of State who are symbols of freedom and also spokesmen for the constitution in our countries. Not only in general, but particularly in the ongoing process of engraving the promises of the constitution in the hearts of their people. This is a very special historical gift that spurs both our countries on to creativity and determination in the defence of what we won with so much suffering.

I know that my congratulations to you on your, as I speak, one hundred and fifty year old constitution and the fifty three year old freedom is coloured by the youthful ebullience of someone who only recently saw his country stand up for a new future. There might well be the odd cynic who could accuse me of romantic exaggeration, perhaps even justifiably. But I wish each and every one of you in your own lives, whatever your position in the community, the invigorating joy of freedom. This is the elation that helped ex-prisoners in South Africa tackle the hard realities of the contemporary situation. I began with a few memories of my own imprisonment and the dreams of my friends in prison. Even as they looked death in the eyes, they did not hesitate to weave deeds out of their dreams.

Your dreamers might be older and further back in history, but the prosperity of the country would be unthinkable without them. To celebrate freedom and to mark the birthday of the constitution is to be prepared to renew the community. With freedom always in mind and the constitution as foundation we must tackle an uncertain future and the continuing demands of renewed commitment with a valiant spirit.

Translation Catherine Knox

Abdul Sheriff

# The Slave Trade and Slavery in the Western Indian Ocean: Significant Contrasts

In a book focused particularly on the Atlantic system of slavery, it may be useful to look as well at the other side of Africa facing the Indian Ocean, to take note of similarities and contrasts that may help in the understanding of this sad chapter in the history of mankind. The slave trade is one of the oldest branches of commerce, but it has hitherto been seen largely through eyes conditioned by the terrible experience of one of its latest chapters, that of Atlantic slavery. On the other hand, in the build-up to the European colonial expansion, the Indian Ocean experience has invariably been associated ideologically with Arabs and Islam to provide a justification for colonialism and Christian missionary activities.

However, slavery is a form of social oppression and economic exploitation that is not confined to any religion or race, and where it prevails, it entangles everybody and every aspect of society. While the slave trade in the Indian Ocean never rivalled the annual volume of the Atlantic trade, the British imperial historian Coupland attributed Africa's 'primitiveness' to the Asian slave trade.[1] There has been an enormous increase in historical research on the postcolonial period, but often without a change in the paradigm. Thus, Austen tries to carry out a census of what he calls the 'Islamic' slave trade – note, however, that the Atlantic slave trade is never equated with Christianity. Although there are hardly any quantitative data from before the nineteenth century, he nevertheless arrives at a total for the slave trade to Asia which unsurprisingly far exceeds Curtin's minimized total for the Atlantic slave trading.[2]

The earliest reference to the slave trade in the Western Indian Ocean goes back to the beginning of the Christian era when slaves were taken from the Horn of Africa to Egypt. Domestic slavery was prevalent in pre-Islamic Arabia, and one of the African slaves, Antar, became a national hero, still popular in contemporary Arabic theatre. Another African slave was Bilal, who was among the earliest converts to Islam. Islam did not justify or abolish slavery, but tried

---

[1] R. Coupland, *East Africa and Its Invaders* (Oxford 1938).

[2] R. Austen, 'The Islamic Slave Trade out of Africa (Red Sea and Indian Ocean). An Effort at Quantification', Paper presented at Conference on Islamic Africa: Slavery and Related Institutions, Princeton, 1977.

to ameliorate and regulate domestic slavery with specific legislation and exhortations on the treatment of slaves. As Mazrui points out, Islamic slavery was creed-conscious and one of its foremost principles was that 'the most devout is the noblest even if he be a Negress's bastard'. Islamic slavery also considered the freeing of a slave an act of charity and piety and it permitted secondary marriages (inappropriately equated with concubinage) to slave girls, but the offspring of those unions were free children with the full rights of their fathers, and their slave mothers could not be sold but were freed on the death of their masters.[3]

Islamic slavery thus had a built-in process of emancipation. The slave population was constantly drained, creating conditions not only for the perpetuation of the slave trade, but also for social integration and assimilation. It provided a window for upward social mobility, or for what Mazrui called 'ascending miscegenation' – in contrast to the American system in which white slave owners refused to acknowledge the paternity of their children born of slave mothers, thereby exacerbating racial consciousness and distance – and even when finally emancipated, they remained a segregated community.[4]

It is ironic that Harris, who was the first African American historian to write on slavery in the Indian Ocean, should lament this 'slow and agonising process of racial and cultural oblivion'.[5] The fact is that the process allowed slaves and their descendants to be integrated into a society not fundamentally based on racial purity but on cultural integrity, even though all the pitfalls of racial prejudice were not necessarily avoided, or the ancestry erased from memory. As a carpenter in the Omani dhow port of Sur said, 'four generations of my family were born in Sur, but the fifth was from Africa. After two or three generations they were considered Omani, but even half the government was African – the mother was African and the father was Omani, but all are Arabs.'[6] One prime example is al-Jahiz, the most illustrious Arab prose writer and philosopher of ninth-century Iraq, whose learning was encyclopaedic and his writings prolific

---

3
B. Lewis, *Race and Slavery in the Middle East* (Oxford 1990).

4
A.A. Mazrui, 'Comparative Slavery in Islam, Africa and the West', Paper presented at a Conference on Islamic Thought, Istanbul, 1997.

5
J.E. Harris, *The African Presence in Asia* (London 1971).

6
A. Sheriff, 'The Slave Trade and its Fallout in the Persian Gulf', Paper presented at the Workshop on Slave Systems in Asia and the Indian Ocean, CERINS, University of Avignon, May, 2000.

on almost every branch of knowledge. But he was of African slave ancestry, and he caustically attacked contemporary Arab prejudice against blacks, writing an impassioned treatise entitled 'The pride of the Blacks against the Whites'.[7]

Al-Jahiz was protesting against the intensification of racial oppression and prejudice occasioned by the first massive importation of slaves from different parts of the world to lower Iraq, in order to desalinate the marshlands for agricultural purposes – under atrocious conditions, despite Islamic injunctions. In the ninth century, this eventually led to the famous Zanj Rebellion: a mass social revolt of all oppressed classes against the Umayyad Caliphate – including poor peasants, non-Arab clients and even Bedouins – led by a leader whose grandmother was an Indian slave. The rebels ruled southern Iraq for fourteen years, and although the rebellion was ultimately suppressed, the slaves never returned to the hated marshlands, but were absorbed in the army or in domestic service.[8]

In view of its own dense population, especially its large poor population that bordered on servility, the potential for slave trade to India was more limited, but caste-conscious Hindu society may have been less assimilative. Nevertheless, some Africans of servile origin played important roles in the history of India, even setting up slave dynasties. Among the most illustrious was Malik Ambar (1550-1626) who became a de-facto ruler of Ahmadnagar in southern India. He built mosques and canals, and was described as a 'nucleus of the revival of the cultural traditions of Ahmadnagar'. However, Rashidi makes an important point that one should not automatically assume that any African in the East was there as a result of the slave trade, for Africans were also engaged in legitimate trade throughout the Indian Ocean, such as Baba Ghor, who set up an agate industry in western India; and Swahili traders were found by the Portuguese as far as Malacca.[9]

The second major phase of the slave trade in East Africa began in the eighteenth century. The development of irrigated date plantations in Oman and pearl diving in the Persian Gulf revived the northern branch of the trade. On the other hand, the French, and briefly the Dutch –

---

7
B. Lewis, *Race and Slavery in the Middle East* (Oxford 1990).
8
G.H. Talhami, 'The Zanj rebellion reconsidered', *International Journal of African Historical Studies*, 10, 1977, pp. 443-61.
9
R. Rashidi (ed.), *African Presence in Early Asia* (New Brunswick 1995).

from the last third of the eighteenth century – developed the southern branch to supply their labour-starved colonies in the Southern Indian Ocean islands and at the Cape, which served as an extension of the Atlantic system. Ironically, British efforts to prohibit the export of slaves from East Africa had the effect of transforming the sector from one depending on the export of slaves into one in which slavery itself was indigenized as a system of production along the East African Coast, with a much greater potential for expansion. Thus, contrary to Coupland's assertion of massive exports of slaves to the poor and sparsely populated desert fringes of Arabia and the Persian Gulf, most of the slaves were absorbed in Zanzibar and the East African Coast to produce cloves and sesame seeds for export to Asia and Europe; and simultaneously, to produce a slave society and a mixed population along the coast in which distinctions of race are difficult to demarcate.

During the nineteenth century, only about an eighth of the slaves reaching the coast from the African interior continued to be smuggled to the northern rim of the Indian Ocean, where they were absorbed either as domestics or farm hands in Oman, or as pearl divers in the Persian Gulf. It is interesting that, in contrast to the Atlantic slave trade, where the emphasis was on a preponderance of able-bodied male adults to work on sugar and cotton plantations for immediate productivity, in the Western Indian Ocean there was a fair proportion of males and females in all branches of the slave trade, and they were predominantly youths who could be socialized before they were assigned domestic or productive activities.

Contrary to popular perception, slaves who were exported to the north did not disappear into thin air but left an indelible imprint on Muslim societies around the Indian Ocean (although it is important to bear in mind the vastly different scales of the slave trade in the Atlantic and Indian Oceans). As a result of miscegenation with African secondary wives during the nineteenth century, communities around the Arabian peninsula have been infused with a considerable amount of African blood. Many communities in the Persian Gulf were routinely described as 'hybrid' or as 'a medley of races', but as Villiers was nonchalantly told, they were all Arabs.[10] Secondly, the Muslim system of emancipation had given birth to a free African stratum within these societies long before formal emancipation was implemented by the British in the twentieth century. Although they were integrated, they could not but inject their own

[10] A. Villiers, *Sons of Sinbad* (New York 1940).

contribution into the cultural melting-pot. African presence is very pronounced in popular rituals and folk music, and many Swahili words have entered local dialects.[11]

Nevertheless, social integration is never a completed process, and while Islam deplores racial prejudice, the practice of Muslims has not always conformed to its high ideals. Barth refers to the 'stigma' of slave admixture that still pervades Omani society,[12] and even in Zanzibar one's social origin is sometimes spoken of in hushed undertones. However, in a society which is creed-conscious and culturally proud, where pigmentation does not coincide with social stratification and where assimilation is apparently an attainable ideal, there is great reluctance to open up old wounds. There is a heated debate going on in the United States whether President Jefferson had a child by a slave woman; contrastingly, in the Persian Gulf the fact that a Crown Prince may have had an African slave mother and is very dark, hardly raises an eyebrow.

The question that remains is how we should deal with this great historical wrongdoing against mankind, and how modern society should render tribute to the past and make reparations for it. Desegregation and assimilation in the West has proved to be a blind alley since while it provided opportunities for upward social mobility for some, it alienated these people from the vast majority that continued to languish at the bottom. The highly racist and segregationist Atlantic system has therefore given rise to a militant response that seeks to celebrate racial origin as the only way to regain humanity and self-respect as a group, and to deal on an equal basis with the counterparts across the racial divide. In the case of the highly assimilative Indian Ocean system, especially along the East African Coast and in the Persian Gulf, that racial divide has proved to be extremely amorphous, although social distinctions may be very real. The most humane tribute in this case, it would seem, would be not to rub salt into the wounds of the past by artificially reviving memories and resurrecting racial distinctions, but to achieve complete social emancipation and equality.

---

11
A. Sheriff, 'The Slave Trade and its Fallout in the Persian Gulf', Paper presented at the Workshop on Slave Systems in Asia and the Indian Ocean, CERINS, University of Avignon, May, 2000. E.A. Alpers, 'The African Diaspora in the Northwestern Indian Ocean', *Comparative Studies of South Asia, Africa and the Middle East*, XVII/2, 1997.
12
F. Barth, *Sohar* (Baltimore 1983).

Nigel Worden

# The Forgotten Region: Commemorations of Slavery in Mauritius and South Africa

Current awareness of the historical role played by Europeans in slavery and the slave trade is overwhelmingly focused on the Atlantic world. Yet the Portuguese, Dutch, French and English were also active slavers in the Indian Ocean and Asian worlds. For instance, the Dutch East India Company (*Vereenigde Oost-Indische Compagnie*, or VOC) created the slave societies of the Cape in South Africa and of Mauritius in the South-West Indian Ocean, whilst playing a key role in the intensification of slavery in Batavia (Jakarta) and elsewhere in the East Indies.[1]

However, slavery in the colonies that the VOC founded at the Cape and in Mauritius plays little part in Dutch historical consciousness. The debates over slavery in these regions came about after Dutch control had been ceded to the British in the early nineteenth century, and abolition was part of the process of British slave emancipation in the 1830s. In the case of Mauritius, Dutch rule was brief (1638-58 and 1664-1710), the island coming under French control instead during the eighteenth century. The development of the Mauritian sugar industry, heavily dependent on slave labour, took place after the ending of Dutch involvement in the island. Nonetheless, today in these regions a new awareness of the need to remember the slave past is arising in ways which may yet inform European historical consciousness.

The VOC was itself a key trader in the slaving activities of the South-West Indian Ocean during the seventeenth and eighteenth centuries, supplying its colonies in Mauritius and the Cape with slaves obtained from Mozambique and Madagascar. Slaves were also brought from South and South-east Asia aboard vessels returning to the Netherlands from Batavia and Ceylon.[2] In Dutch Mauritius slave numbers were never large, but maroon slave runaways caused major problems for the VOC.[3] At the Cape, slaves formed the mainstay of the labour force, although the absence of a plantation export crop meant that numbers were smaller than in the Caribbean

---

[1]
J. Fox, '"For Good and Sufficient Reasons". An Examination of Early Dutch East India Company Ordinances on Slaves and Slavery', in: A. Reid (ed.), *Slavery, Bondage and Dependency in South-East Asia* (St Lucia: University of Queensland Press 1983), pp. 246-51.

[2]
J. Armstrong and N. Worden, 'The Slaves, 1652-1834', in: R. Elphick and H. Giliomee (eds), *The Shaping of South African Society, 1652-1840* (Cape Town: Maskew Miller Longman 1989), pp. 110-22.

The National Monument to Slavery

The National Monument to Slavery is expected to be unveiled in Amsterdam's Oosterpark in 2002. Slavery has long been an omitted chapter in the Netherlands' history books. [...] Dutch slavery is not only an essential part of the past, it also affects the present. Both blacks and whites are inheritors of this history. The descendants of slaves carry with them the heritage of their forebears and pass this on to their children, while other people of the Netherlands are often completely unaware that they too are inheritors of this history. The monument will therefore stand as a symbol of slavery history and its effects on our multicultural society today. [...] The Minister of Metropolitan Policy and Integration, Roger van Boxtel, took responsibility for the establishment of a national monument on behalf of the cabinet. The Secretary of State for Culture, Rick van der Ploeg, was also closely involved. Those who took the initiative for the monument, eighteen organizations of Surinamese, Antillian, Aruban and African affiliation, organized themselves into the National Platform for Slavery Past. [...] Nine artists who originate from or live in Suriname, the Antilles, Aruba, West Africa and the Netherlands have been invited to submit a design for the monument. In the following pages, their designs and accompanying explanations are presented. [Extracts from: Brochure about the National Monument to Slavery, Ministry of Education, Culture and Science, Ministry of the Interior and Kingdom Relations, and City Council of Amsterdam, 2001, Translated by A. Howland. Photo's Jørgen Krielen.]

Nelson Carilho (Curaçao, 1953)
*The Road to Freedom*

In order to give the collective past of slavery the status it deserves in the present it is necessary to face up to this period in all its complexity. *The Road to Freedom* offers the spectator a view of the past which emphasizes the future. With this subject the artist aims to inspire the viewer into going one step further in the process of self-liberation and self-awakening; to go beyond the crippling emotions of guilt or shame. This dynamic memorial, a symbolic path, offers the viewer a route to introspection and movement. The journey is manifested in three symbolic elements: the Gateway as view of the future, the Bridge as connection, and the Soul as inner source of strength. These elements are combined with engraved stanzas from slave songs which resonate hope, courage and strength.

Ed van Doorn (the Netherlands, 1941)
*Looking Each Other in the Eye, Facing the Future Together*

Bronze, broken chains on an obelisk represent the past of slavery. The obelisk's length symbolizes the centuries of slavery. The view of the future is depicted through two faces of equal size and features, but one dark and one light, who can and want to look each other in the eye. Their equality is emphasized by the sentence, 'All blood is red'.

Meshac Gaba (Benin, 1961)
*La Route de l'Esclave*

This monument represents the wheel of a ship. The seafarer is depicted on a bench made of wood and concrete. Visitors may sit on this bench facing two directions and decide whether they want to look at the monument or the park. At the centre of the wheel is a representation of the Atlantic in the form of a fountain. In the fountain are depicted different tools of torture dating from the time of slavery. The coins in the fountain come from the countries that were involved in the slave trade. A piece of Africa is visible in the corner of the Atlantic Ocean. Different objects are scattered on this piece of land. These objects were used as loose change in the selling of slaves. Visitors cannot leave the monument through the entrance they came in through; slaves couldn't return to their countries of origin after the abolition of slavery.

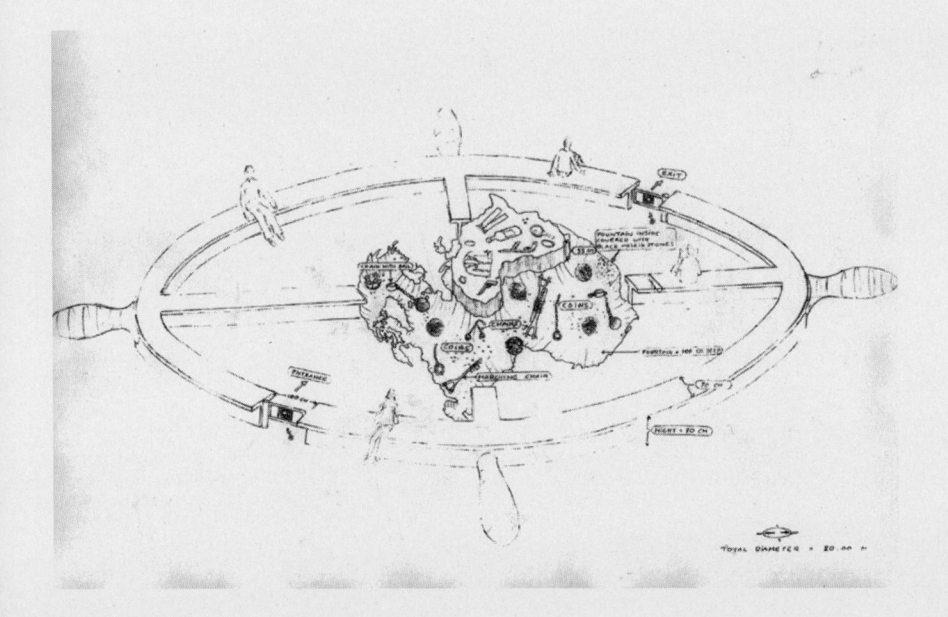

Glenda Heyliger (Aruba)
*Untitled*

This design consists of two glass pillars which are twisted together. The twisting of the pillars represents 'bending over backwards', breaking with the established order and the past to make room for reconciliation. The interlinked form also represents the collective past and present. At the top is a universal heart. This heart represents solidarity. Hearts float inside the transparent columns. The red hearts presented in the model will be real hearts in a preserving liquid in the final monument. The hearts bear the names of slaves who fought for the liberation of the slaves. With these organs the artist wants to draw attention to our bodily functions and thereby our vulnerability. The heart represents physical and emotional vulnerability and feeling. The preservation of the organs symbolizes the slaves' personalities and their stories which, despite everything else, were never taken from them.

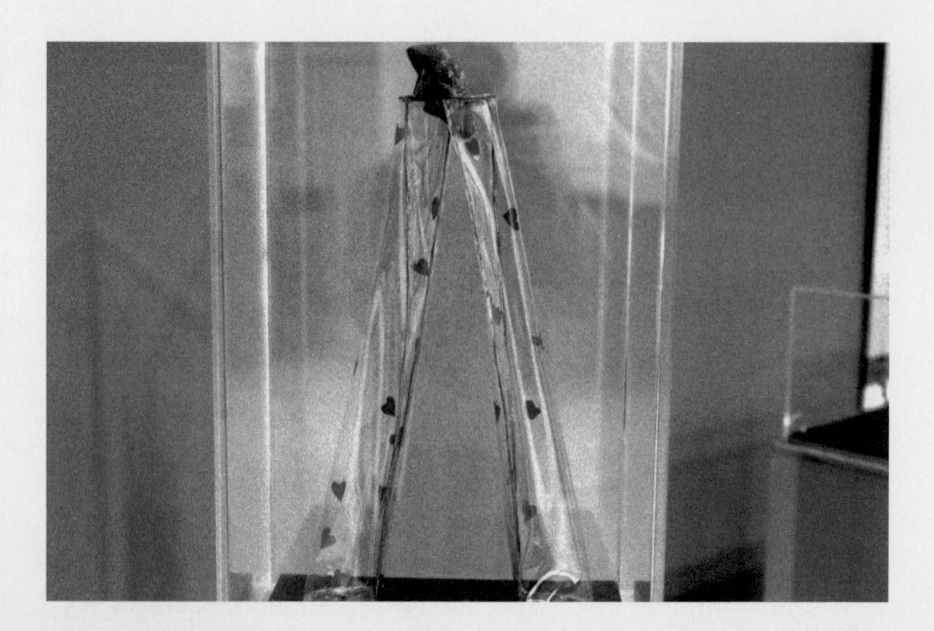

Designs for the National Monument to Slavery in the Netherlands xv

Remy Jungerman (Suriname, 1959)
*United, 'A people without the knowledge of their past history, origin and culture is like a tree without roots'.*

The monument contains spaces both above and below ground. On the round plateau above the ground stands a metal megaphone painted in cobalt blue. The blue refers to purification. On an elevated part of the platform is a steel ring. When the ring is moved upwards a mechanical system sets a number of metal tubes in motion so that they knock together and generate sound. The aluminium tubes are housed in the underground space. When the ring is replaced is may be used as a doorknocker, a symbol for making contact or saying goodbye. The visitor plays an active part in the monument. It should be a place where, through sound, people may contemplate and reflect upon the injustices people were and are subjected to. The monument should evoke a sense of peace for the descendants of slaves, providing them with a space to honour their forebears.

Soheila Najand (Iran, 1959)
*Untitled*

This memorial is a transparent ship made from perspex which evokes ice. The transparency is metaphorical: the viewer can look through the ship and thus through history. Inside the ship drawers are visible in which human figures occasionally move, literally forming a living memory. To emphasize that their spirits are still present, texts light up periodically. The static yet dynamic character of the monument allows the viewer to truly sense the relationship between the past, the present and the future.

Gerald Steven Pinedo (Curaçao, 1958)
*Untitled*

This monument consists of a partially stripped ship's hull, a beacon of the descendants' struggle against all kinds of inhumanity, racism and oppression. The ship also expresses positive realization and calls our society to fight against injustice. The monument is a ship where there is room for everyone. The ship is positioned in the middle of a boulder-filled circle, which can be regarded as a protective ring, 'a sign of God'. The circle protects the ship, a symbol of the battle against racism. The magic circle is a symbol that was taken by slaves from Africa. The boulders in the circle serve as a foundation out of which the ship emerges. The many stones represent the countless lives that were taken by slavery.

XVIII  Designs for the National Monument to Slavery in the Netherlands

Nel Simon (Curaçao, 1938)
*Goddess, Mother Africa*

This monument has three levels. At the centre of the highest plateau are two bronze and two stone sculptures. The two stone sculptures are in the shapes of Suriname and the island of Madagascar. On the plateau underneath are two more stone sculptures in the shapes of the islands of the Netherlands Antilles and Aruba. Together these four stone sculptures symbolize the links between these peoples. One of the bronze sculptures, Goddess, Mother Africa, symbolizes the African roots shared by the descendants of the slaves from Suriname, the Netherlands Antilles and Aruba. The other bronze sculpture, an obelisk, consists of two, partially unrolled, rolls of parchment, which together form a triangle. The triangle symbolizes the three-way relation between the Netherlands, Africa and the Americas, and the route taken by the slave ships. On the rolls is also a relief of the sankofa bird of Ghana. The sankofa bird is an African symbol for wisdom, indicating the necessity of knowing and studying one's own past in order to be able to determine one's own path in the future.

Erwin de Vries (Suriname, 1929)
*Untitled*

In its entirety this design represents the past, present and future. It consists of three elements. The element at the rear symbolizes the dramatic history of the yoke which bore down on the slaves. In the middle element humanity breaks through the wall of resistance and taboo. People have found the strength to free themselves of chains to be able to stand upright as fully-fledged individuals in the present. The front element of the design underlines the predominant drive for freedom and a better future which every individual possesses.

colonies (approximately 20,000 at the end of VOC rule in 1795). On the pastoral farms of the interior, Cape slaves also worked alongside indigenous Khoisan serfs.

Under British rule, slavery was abolished in both colonies in the 1830s. In Mauritius they were replaced on the sugar estates by indentured labour imported from India, and reduced by the late nineteenth century to a marginal position as subsistence cultivators and dockworkers in Port Louis. At the Cape there was no such substitute supply of labour, and freed slaves and their descendants have continued to this day to form the mainstay of the rural and urban labour force of the Western Cape province of South Africa.[4]

In both Mauritius and the Cape, public memory of the slave past has been obscured and suppressed. In Mauritius the domination of Indians in the post-emancipation economy and in the politics of independence in the 1960s, obscured the heritage of slave descendants. In the ethnically-determined electoral classification system of independent Mauritius, this remains characterized by the inclusion of Afro-Mauritians (or 'Creoles') as part of the 'General Population', lumped together with the Franco-Mauritian elite, in opposition to the distinct categories of 'Moslem', 'Hindu' and 'Sino-Mauritian'. Many slave descendants sided with the descendants of their masters, the Franco-Mauritians, in opposing independence in 1968 on the grounds that the new state would be dominated by Indian Mauritians who would not represent their interests.

Under such circumstances it is not surprising that slavery played little part in the forging of a Mauritian nationalist history. Recognition by local historians of the slave past only came at the time of the 150th anniversary of abolition in 1985.[5] An African Cultural Centre was established, although it received little funding or support from the state. But in the 1990s, the economic, social and political 'exclusion' of many slave descendants was a burning issue in Mauritius and became a key campaign of the opposition party, the *Mouvement Militant Mauricien* (MMM).

In September 1998, the Mauritian government held major celebrations to commemorate the 400th anniversary of the Dutch 'discovery' of Mauritius in 1598. Members of the Dutch Royal Family paid a state visit, monuments were unveiled and an academic conference held. But the

[3] P.J. Moree, *A Concise History of Dutch Mauritius, 1598-1710* (London and New York: Kegan Paul International 1998), p. 37.

[4] R. Ross, '"Rather mental than physical". Emancipations and the Cape Economy', in: N. Worden and C. Crais (eds), *Breaking the Chains. Slavery and its Legacy in the Nineteenth Century Cape Colony* (Johannesburg: Witwatersrand University Press 1994), pp. 145-67.

[5] U. Bissoondoyal and S.B.C. Servansing (eds), *Slavery in the South-West Indian Ocean* (Moka: Mohatma Gandhi Institute 1989).

descendants of slaves were critical of such celebrations. Creole artists from Mauritius and Reunion held their own ceremonies to mark the memory of the slaves who had first arrived with the Dutch at sites of significance to their slave heritage.[6] Posters appeared on the streets written in Creole stating:

> '1598: arrival of the african slave
> 1998: we are still squatters when will we be free?'

> 'after 400 years the creole community are still excluded
> 1836: the visible chains become invisible'

In this view 'emancipation' was not true emancipation at all.

Just two weeks after the Dutch celebrations, the UNESCO 'Slave Route' project held a conference in Port Louis, to draw attention to the history of slavery and its impact on modern Mauritius. The municipality of Port Louis was under the control of the MMM party, and although the conference grudgingly obtained government backing, it was clearly a political initiative by the opposition party. The mayors of Maputo (Mozambique), La Possession (Réunion), and Dakar (Senegal) – all places from which slaves had been brought to Mauritius – were invited and a special monument was unveiled to the 'Unknown Slave'. Resolutions passed by the conference

---

[6] V.Y. Hookoomsing, 'Identités ... (ré)construire: points de repère culturel', Paper presented at Colloque sur L'Esclavage et ses Séquelles; Mémoire et Vécu d'Hier et d'Aujourd'hui, Port Louis, 5-8 October 1998, p. 2.

Creole Protest posters, Rose-Hill, Mauritius, 1998 (N. Worden).

included the establishment of a slavery museum in Port Louis, calls for the replacement of the 'General Population' electoral category by one of 'Creoles' only, the establishment of 1 February as a public holiday, the inclusion of materials on slavery in the Mauritian school curriculum and a demand for reparations. The latter included demands for funding by the past colonial powers (the Netherlands, Britain and France) for Creole housing and education and compensation by these powers to the Mauritian government.[7]

Yet, although the Mauritian Prime Minister's opening speech at the conference also called for reparations for slavery, after two years little had been done. Instead, further controversy flared when in late 1999 developers, with state backing, planned to build a cable car on Le Morne, a spectacular mountain overlooking the sea, which had been occupied by slave runaways in the eighteenth and early nineteenth centuries and which is reputed in local oral traditions to be the site of slave suicides. In response to protest by local academics and community organizers, the developers offered to fund archaeological excavation at Le Morne, but only on a temporary basis and on condition that tourist development would still go ahead. The election of a new coalition government with MMM participation in late 2000 has led to some greater recognition of a slave heritage. February 1, 2001 was declared a national holiday in commemoration of emancipation. But hitherto (April 2001) no decision has been made about the future of Le Morne and it remains to be seen whether the site will be protected against the strong lure of tourist development projects.

In South Africa, memories and public evocations of slavery are similarly complex. Up until very recently, little of the legacy of Cape slavery had appeared in the public memory of the country.[8] This was partly the result of the suppression of the history of South Africa's black, marginalized and working class people which pervaded the school curricula, museum representations and public history of the apartheid era. But in the alternative popular histories and memories evoked in the 1970s and 1980s in resistance to apartheid, Cape slavery also played little part. There were good political reasons for this. Chattel slavery had been confined to one region of the country, the Western Cape. Cape slavery had little to offer South Africans elsewhere in the country who

[7] Resolutions 1998. Colloque, L'Esclavage et ses Séquelles. Mémoire et Vécu d'Hier et d'Aujourd'hui, Port Louis, 10 October 1998.
[8] K. Ward and N. Worden, 'Commemorating, Suppressing and Invoking Cape slavery', in: S. Nuttall and C. Coetzee (eds), *Negotiating the Past. The Making of Memory in South Africa* (Cape Town: Oxford University Press 1997), pp. 201-17.

were seeking to recapture a past which white rule had denied them. And in the Western Cape itself, slavery was also seen as divisive; a history which, 'in the struggle', separated 'Coloured' South Africans from their brothers and sisters who descended from indigenous inhabitants of the land.

In the past few years, however, the Cape's slave heritage is beginning to be recovered in ways which reflect the new realities of the post-apartheid era. At one level this is apparent in the use of the recent work of slave historians and archaeologists in school curricula and in the beginnings of a reorientation of museum displays to incorporate the slave past. It is also apparent in a new public awareness of a slave heritage, harnessed to current needs and concerns. For instance, in 1995 and 1996 there were calls for a new political organization to represent coloured interests, arising from the rejection of the ANC by many coloured voters in both national and municipal elections. The 'December 1 Movement' (named after Slave Emancipation Day) was founded by a group of middle class coloureds (clergy, academics and politicians) who were frustrated at the lack of a forum for political and economic issues faced by coloureds in the Western Cape region. On 1 December 1996 its launch was accompanied by the laying of a wreath at the site in central Cape Town where slave auctions were believed to have been held.[9] But the December 1 Movement swiftly attracted criticism for evoking a separatist ethnic identity which divided 'our own blood brothers and comrades' of the recent past.[10] Although there were attempts to revive the movement, it was actively opposed by both the ANC and the National Party, attracted little corporate funding and has now sunk without trace.

The ambiguities of an appeal to a slave heritage in post-apartheid South Africa was further revealed by the government's response to the UNESCO 'Slave Route' project. Local researchers and tour guides saw the 'Slave Route' as a public commemoration of the specific institution of Cape slavery, particularly designed to empower local communities of slave descent. However, central government representatives insisted that slavery be seen as part of a broader 'South African nation-building exercise' and that it should include 'such issues as indentured labour, forced migration, convict and farm labour'.[11] The current stress of the South African government on 'nation-building' means that any heritage which is only local could be anathema, parti-

[9] *Cape Times*, 'December 1st movement reveals plans', 21 October 1996.

[10] G. Mamputa, Letter to *Cape Times*, 23 October 1996.

cularly when it might be interpreted as an evocation of 'Coloured' ethnic identity, which is widely believed to have led to repeated ANC electoral defeats in the Western Cape.

However, local initiatives continued. On Heritage Day (24 September) 1998 the South African Cultural History Museum, housed in the building where VOC slaves were kept, was renamed the 'Slave Lodge'. At a well-attended ceremony dramatic evocations of the building's slave past were presented and commemorative candles lit for each year of the existence of slavery at the Cape. Sites of slave significance have been identified. Hopes of economic benefit to be derived from cultural tourism encouraged some local communities to recover a slave heritage. This is most striking at Elim mission station, some 150 kilometres from Cape Town, a place to which many freed slaves moved at the time of emancipation. In late 2000 the potential for tourism has encouraged the Western Cape local government (which is under the control of the national opposition Democratic Alliance) to plan a local 'Slave Route', although such initiatives are still in their very early stages.

But such evocations of the slave past in the Western Cape region have not formed part of a national identity and have lacked the stridency of calls for reparations from previous colonial rulers of the kind taking place in Mauritius. In South Africa the identified enemy of the past is not the Dutch or the British, but rather the local settler apartheid state whose machinations were publicly revealed through the evidence given to the Truth and Reconciliation Commission. Compensation and redress for the evils of apartheid currently override calls for reparations for slavery. Where a remoter past has been evoked in this context, it is by First People movements calling for restoration of land, although this is also a demand made to the current South African government, not to the ex-colonial powers such as the Dutch. In October 2001 an international conference on Race and Reparations for Slavery and Colonialism will be held in Durban, and it is envisaged that calls will be made there for redress for the history of slavery. However, this will be together with other broader themes, such as colonialism and racism in general and it remains to be seen whether the specifics of Cape slavery or Dutch responsibility will be highlighted.

In 1952, the 300th anniversary of the Dutch founding of the Cape, the official Van Riebeeck Festival celebrations (which were fully supported by the Dutch government) were boycotted by

---

11
UNESCO 1997. Report of a National Conference of the South African Chapter of the UNESCO Slave Route Project held at Robben Island, 24-26 October 1997, p. 4.

anti-apartheid groups within the country. Yet in the representations of both the festival organizers and those of their opponents, Van Riebeeck's landing, and with it the VOC Dutch heritage of the Cape, was turned into a founding symbol of a local, not a colonial, history.[12] Slavery, colonialism and racism, attributed to Van Riebeeck, became identified with the local settler and apartheid state. Later Dutch support for the anti-apartheid movement also to a large extent removed its association with its colonial past in South Africa.

South African national identity thus has less need for strong antagonism towards the Dutch in the way that has taken place, for example, in Suriname,[13] or which is currently being identified by some Afro-Mauritians. But this issue is now coming to the fore with current discussions over South African participation in the commemorations in 2002 of the 400th anniversary of the founding of the VOC – a date which coincides with the 350th anniversary of Dutch colonization of the Cape in 1652. A mission statement by the local committee of this project identifies the VOC with colonial rule and calls for recognition of the heritage of those brought by the Dutch to South Africa 'against their will'. However, government support towards such a commemoration has been ambivalent, and by the end of 2000 no state support was forthcoming. Instead, plans are being made for a privately-funded exhibition in Cape Town Castle which will include displays on Cape slavery.

It remains to be seen whether the VOC 2002 celebrations, which will take place in the Netherlands, will record the role of the Dutch in the creation of slave societies in Mauritius and the Cape. If so, they will provide the first public acknowledgment in Europe of responsibility for slaving activities in the Indian Ocean. However, current signs do not give cause for optimism in this regard.

[12]
C. Rassool and L. Witz, 'The 1952 Jan van Riebeeck Tercentenary Festival: Constructing and Contesting Public National History in South Africa', *Journal of African History*, 34, 1993, pp. 447-68.

[13]
G.J. Oostindie, *Het paradijs overzee. De 'Nederlandse' Caraïben en Nederland* (Amsterdam: Bert Bakker 1997), pp. 305-26.

The Americas

# Ina Césaire

## To Each His Commemoration

In Martinique the opinions and analyses of the anniversary of the abolition of slavery are so varied that a detailed typology is called for.

1.
'The naive response': this attitude, far from giving in to the current craze, does not understand why we should commemorate the end of a system that, aside from its excesses, brought happiness and a better life. It is due to the system of servitude that black Africans escaped barbarism and were introduced to the true religion through the missionaries; and by learning the dominant language gained access to the higher echelons of the social hierarchy.

2.
'The positive response': this attitude suffers neither the heavy analysis nor the weak ideology of the first. It recognizes, however, that slavery, although regrettable because of its barbarism, led to very positive effects by creating: a) a wonderful country (the Antilles); b) a beautiful race, the Creoles, with stunning women who have become beauty queens admired everywhere; c) high level athletes; d) brilliant artists, writers, musicians, etc.

3.
'The forgetful response': this attitude prefers to turn the page and not look back. Like the proverbial ostrich with its head in the sand, it believes that talking about slavery – and a fortiori commemorating it – comes down to a) masochism; b) racism, by reminding a white Europe of the abomination committed by long ago ancestors; c) a lack of Christian charity by refusing to forgive.

4.
'The vengeful response': this attitude is openly vindicative, not hiding its rancour towards the white planters and wealthy blacks who were the toast of such cities as Nantes or Liverpool. It believes that the slave trade and slavery robbed individuals of their original country and their grasp of the future. It demands reparations (frequently drawing a comparison to the holocaust of the Jews).

5.
'The moralist response': this attitude demands symbolic compensation. It is moved by a philosophical approach that is often channelled into artistic creation. Without bitterness, but

with firmness, it calls for a) the descendants of former criminals to recognize slavery as a crime against humanity; and b) the descendants of former victims to go through required exercises of 'remembrance'.

6.

'The don't worry, be happy response': this local attitude is expressed by those who do not want to be burdened with sad memories or vengeful recriminations or disturbing claims. This anniversary is supposed to be a festival that shows once again our pleasure-loving and uncomplicated nature.

7.

'The serene response' has a philosophy, be it secular or religious, that believes there are reasons to hope that justice will erase the consequences of an unhappy past. It believes in human fraternity and tends to consider racism as an obsolete phenomenon.

8.

'The outsider response' is that of those who come generally from the former colonizing country and commonly enjoy some sort of official financing. Looking steadfastly into the future, this group does not wish to dwell on the past. Surrounded by researchers and specialists, the outsider declaims economic factors underlying slavery and the slave trade, analysing in depth the 'plantation system' or the 'sugar economy'.

This typological matrix is not at all exhaustive and could be applied without any trouble to each paragraph. In our country, there are many people who wish to make this anniversary a commemoration and not a celebration. I am not among those who accept the arguments about diminishing the social impact of this inconceivable historical atrocity. If we as Antillians have a responsibility to the coming generations, it is the responsibility of remembrance that constitutes the minimum guarantee against possible reoccurrence. If we demand recognition of the slave trade and slavery as a crime against humanity, we do so to preserve an essential bit of our dignity.

Translation Elisabeth Daverman

Richard Price

## Monuments and Silent Screamings: A View from Martinique[1]

*'If we forget the deeds of our ancestors, how can we hope to avoid being returned to whitefolks' slavery?'*

[Overheard] One Saramaka Maroon addressing another, Suriname, 1970s.

At this *fin-de-siècle*, metropolitan newspapers recount story after story of the guilt of nations – Germany wrestling with class action suits about slave labour under the Nazis, Japan apologizing successfully to Korea but unsuccessfully to China for wartime atrocities, Switzerland settling out of court for plundered bank holdings. In some cases apologies seem to suffice, in others they are complemented by cash, and in still others by monuments, museums, or foundations to memorialize this or that atrocity.[2]

Regarding the transatlantic slave trade and slavery, the acceptance of national responsibility has been far more muted. Since the 1960s, independent countries with citizens of slave ancestry have raised countless memorials to rebellion – slaves breaking their chains are most common, as in Haiti, Guyana, Barbados and Suriname – and have rewritten colonial schoolbooks to retell history at least in part from a non-imperial view. From Cuba to Brazil, there has been a renaissance of scholarly and popular interest in slavery (particularly in resistance), beginning at last to come to grips with its determinant role in the forging of American nations. Likewise, under the impetus of the Civil Rights Movement, the United States has witnessed a remarkable wave of

---

[1] This paper was written in 1998 as a contribution to Dutch discussions on a monument in commemoration of slavery, and therefore contains some specific references to that particular year and to the Dutch situation.

[2] In a penetrating essay on history, memory and public commemoration, Tony Judt notes that 'We are living through an era of commemoration. Throughout Europe and the United States, memorials, monuments, commemorative plaques, and sites are being erected to remind us of our heritage.... We commemorate many more things; we disagree over what should be commemorated, and how; and whereas until recently (in Europe at least) the point of a museum, a memorial plaque, or a monument was to remind people of what they already knew or thought they knew, today these things serve a different end. They are there to tell people about things they may not know, things they have forgotten or never learned. We live in growing fear that we shall forget the past, that it will somehow get misplaced among the bric-a-brac of the present.... [But] in erecting formal reminders or replicas of something we ought to remember, we risk further forgetfulness: by making symbols or remnants stand for the whole, we ease ourselves into an illusion. In James Young's words, "Once we assign monumental form to memory, we have to some degree divested ourselves of the obligation to remember.... Under the illusion that our memorial edifices will always be there to remind us, we take leave of them and return only at our convenience."' (Tony Judt, 'A la Recherche du Temps Perdu', *New York Review of Books*, 3 December 1998).

slavery studies; memories of slavery – once awash with collective shame for both blacks and whites – have become part of the consciousness of every North American, and for many descendants of the survivors a badge of solidarity and pride.

The European record has been rather more spotty and dependent on modalities of decolonization, numbers of immigrants from former plantation colonies, and national proclivities toward arrogance or humility. In this context, recent Dutch self-examination and collective guilt – even if in part prompted by a wave of new immigrants – hardly surprises.

In their 150th anniversary year of the abolition of slavery, the French, though they have more than once tried to equate emancipation with national generosity, have also showed a modicum of public recognition that, like their European brethren, their ancestors played a significant role in the trade. Under sponsorship of the socialist government, memorials have been sprouting up in every corner of the empire. On the Indian Ocean island of Réunion, when France's *Secrétaire d'État à l'Outre-mer* inaugurated the first of twenty-four planned slavery memorials (one in each *commune*), he noted in his speech that 'the government has at last decided to end its silence' about the French role in slavery and that 'the minister of national education has decided to introduce slavery into the teaching of history, both in the metropole and in overseas France'.[3]

At the *mairie* of Anses d'Arlet – the small Martiniquan town where I live – a travelling commemorative exhibition is now on view: '150 years of Abolition – 1848-1998'. The exhibit opens with a photo of a petition to the International Court of Justice in the Hague, signed by leading French Caribbean intellectuals (Glissant, Chamoiseau), solemnly asking that the slave trade and slavery be officially declared 'a crime against humanity'. The exhibition itself, prepared by Martiniquan scholars, is broken into ten sections covering 'The Trade', 'Profits', 'The Men', 'The Hell of the Plantation', 'The Difficulties of Freedom', and so forth. Yet of the many photos and engravings displayed, there is not a single one of a slave in the French Antilles (only slaves in Brazil, North Africa and elsewhere). And the four panels in *L'enfer de l'habitation* treat 1. 'the Eastern trade' – slavery in Egypt and North Africa –, 2. resistance to slavery in Mauritania and elsewhere in North Africa today, 3. 'After 1848' – Chinese labourers in Cuba, the abolition of slavery in Brazil –, and 4. French colonization in Africa. There is not a single word on plantation slavery in Martinique or Guadeloupe (neither about slaves nor masters) – as if this exhibition

[3]
'Inauguration d'un Mémorial aux esclaves par Jean-Jack Queyranne', *France-Antilles*, 21 décembre 1998, p. 8.

were designed to commemorate a 'crime against humanity' that indeed happened, but that happened 'somewhere else'. (But remember, as Trouillot points out, that 'Martinique, a tiny territory less than one-fourth the size of Long Island, imported more slaves than all the U.S. states combined'[4], making it arguably the slave society *par excellence*. And also that today more than ninety per cent of the population is descended, at least in part, from these slaves, whilst many of the others descended exclusively from their *béké* masters.)

During the past few months the neighbouring town of Diamant has erected not one but two commemorative monuments – the first, like that of countless other *communes* in the French Antilles, representing the 'Neg' Marron' (the mythical Maroon, who holds such a central place in the Antillean literary imagination), the second the African victims of a nineteenth-century shipwreck just off the coast. (See page II, III). Our fishermen friends see both as consummate wastes of taxpayer money. And the realist-style Maroon, they complain, doesn't look sufficiently 'African' (i.e. savage) – indeed, they say, he looks like 'a (modern) Martiniquan' – while the symbolic human figures in the shipwreck memorial are carved from white stone rather than black. Besides, they ask, why dwell on slavery, a shameful period long-since gone?

For Caribbean peoples – fisherfolk, peasants, town-dwellers – history (with slavery at the centre) has often seemed a nightmare best forgotten. With the significant exception of Maroons (and perhaps rural Haitians), the silencing of the past has been endemic. Local intellectuals have long recognized this collective amnesia among 'the folk'. Césaire writes of 'this land without stela, these paths without memory', Glissant of 'the loss of collective memory, the careful erasure of the past', Walcott that 'In time, the slave surrendered to amnesia [and] that amnesia is the true history of the New World', and Patterson that 'The most important legacy of slavery is the total break, not with the past so much as with a consciousness of the past. To be a West Indian is to live in a state of utter pastlessness.' Writing about the Caribbean in general, George Lamming has recently pointed out that the tremendous growth in scholarly knowledge about resistance to slavery 'still awaits mass distribution, and, therefore, has not yet become the shaping influence on the consciousness of those whose recent ancestors had made it possible. It is not inscribed in consciousness.'[5]

One challenge then, is how to bring this knowledge, and its significance, to the descendants of

---

[4] Michel-Rolph Trouillot, *Silencing the Past* (Boston: Beacon Press 1995), p. 17.

the millions brought to the New World as slaves, to the descendants of those who – however much at arm's length – trafficked in human flesh (and, in some cases, continue to profit directly from the economic arrangements plantation slavery established), and to the rest of humanity. In much of the Americas, slavery remains a festering wound at once shameful and dangerous, and its legacies – despite official silencing – are everywhere. In this context, it seems to me, neither petitions nor monuments are quite sufficient. Indeed, if Walcott is right in asking 'Who in the New World does not have a horror of the past, whether his ancestor was torturer or victim? Who, in the depth of conscience, is not silently screaming for pardon or for revenge?'[6] we (as intellectuals, scholars and writers) might begin by accepting our responsibilities to better analyze the reasons for this continued silent screaming. After all, the 'guestbook' at the Anses d'Arlet exhibit – the one that never specifically mentions the horrors of local slavery or even the existence of the local planter class – nevertheless includes numerous scrawled comments, some in Creole, saying 'Shame on [or Death to] the *békés!*'

Teaching the Caribbean (or better, the Atlantic) past *in all its complexities* might be our most important task, both through continued scholarly work and by relentless popularization of that knowledge, in elementary school books, in highschool texts, and through other media. As we now know, the Atlantic slave trade and plantation slavery caused the greatest forced migration in human history, changed the face of four continents, and altered forever the world economic order. Despite several decades of intensive work, which have turned up remarkable new resources for the interpretation of slavery, the ongoing legacies of the institution are still only partly understood and appreciated. This research and outreach remains our central responsibility for the twenty-first century.

My thoughts on memorials run less to bricks and mortar than to knowledge and its diffusion. What if we tried to make sure that every schoolchild in Europe, the Americas and Africa is exposed as fully as possible to the history of slavery and the complexity of its legacy? And if something more particularly Dutch is called for, something more concrete, perhaps the construction of one or more libraries – with exhibition rooms and space for theatre and dance –

5
Sources for these quotations and, in some cases further extensions of them, may be found in Richard Price, *The Convict and the Colonel* (Boston: Beacon Press 1998), pp. 166-9.
6
Derek Walcott, 'The Muse of History', in: Orde Coombs (ed.), *Is Massa Day Dead?* (New York: Anchor 1974), p. 4.

makes most sense. Not dead spaces but live ones, in which scholars, artists and schoolchildren could continually build on the everchanging knowledge of the past to find new meanings for the present. Shelves of books on which the words of Dutch slave masters and African slaves, of Moravian missionaries and heroic Maroons intermingle. Monuments against silencing, places of continuing exploration and expression. Works in progress that respect the past and can hope, therefore, to transcend it.

Postscript on the dangers of banalization and tokenism. As I finish these paragraphs on New Year's Day, I attend the annual reception at the Anses d'Arlet *mairie*. The mayor speaks solemnly of the year gone by, mentioning the triumph of pluri-ethnicity in France's winning World Cup soccer team and evoking the importance of the petition to declare slavery a crime against humanity. And then, after offering a plastic glass of champagne to each citizen, the mayor presents each with a gift – a silver key chain with attached medallion, on one face the town viewed from the sea, on the other a symbolic rendering of Liberty, with the inscription: '150 Anniversaire Abolition de l'Esclavage – 1848-1998'.

Pedro Pérez Sarduy

## In Living Memory: The Commemoration of Slavery in Cuba

I loved my Great-gran Sabue[1], my mother's gran, a lot. She wasn't really called Sabue, that's what I called her because she didn't like Cunduna, her real name, and to call her Great-gran didn't seem affectionate enough to me. She said she wasn't called Cunduna either, but she couldn't remember her real name. That's why, rather than Cunduna or Great-gran, I preferred to call her Sabue, and she seemed to like it, also because I was the only one who called her that. Sabue lived down by the marsh, on the outskirts of Quemado de Güines, a small rural town in the north of Las Villas province[2] which had big sugar cane plantations, and we lived in the provincial capital Santa Clara.

When my mother and I went to the end-of-year festivities – December 24, Christmas Eve, and December 26, *Quemadense Ausente*[3], a day to honour those who had been born there and gone off to the capital – Sabue would come to fetch me early in the morning and I'd spend most of the day with her, in her shack. I'd help her make wood charcoal to sell, amongst other things. We always had some excuse for being together. I learnt a lot on those visits. At the beginning, it was once a year, but after my parents separated and my mother had to go to Havana to work as a servant, and I had to go and live with Aunt Nena – the oldest of my mother's nine sisters, who lived in Quemado – I was happy that we could be together two or three times a month. Sabue didn't much like going into town, as people made fun of her and called her names because she wore clothes of many colours and a white turban. I remember how she'd say people had to respect her because she was *negra de nación*, a black African nation woman. She'd repeat this with great authority, but gently and in syncopated cadence.

We all knew from her that she had come as a small child with her mother as a slave, from a far-off place called Africa. She never mentioned dates, but events that had occurred: 'Mama died of typhoid in the slave quarters, during the rains before the harvest.' When her mind was clear, Sabue, with her stock of many years of life, told me 'black slave things', so I'd know about colonial times, when there were many slaves in Cuba and blacks wanted an end to slavery once and for

---

[1] A derivative from the Spanish *bisabuela*, meaning great-grandmother.
[2] Today Villa Clara province.
[3] The Absent Quedadense (person from Quemado).

all, but there was no end to the overseer's whip. Of course, she had her own way of telling. If anyone or anything crossed her, Sabue would stand tall and thin, one hand raising her old carved ebony stick, the other on her waist, and declare in a serious tone, in her Bantu manner, if not language: 'Don't mess with Cunduna, I'm *negra gangá de nación*[4], damn it.'

Sabue's only daughter was my grandmother Alberta, who I called Tata. It was upon overhearing, years later, my mother and some of her many sisters talking, that I learnt that Sabue had made a papaya seed remedy to have no more children. Sabue told me, without much of an explanation, that she'd had to work hard for my gran not to be a slave. It so happens Tata was born around 1875, five years after the Spanish authorities declared the 'free belly' law of 1870, whereby the children of slave mothers were no longer considered captive.

I was never a naughty child, but, like all children, got into trouble now and then – I'd throw stones at the mango trees, I'd go hunting snakes and *hutias* in neighbours' yards, looking for snails, scorpions and all kinds of strange bugs to play with. When I'd get into mischief, Sabue would tell me off: 'You little devil… you're worse than Aponte.' She'd say it kindly, because she knew José Antonio Aponte hadn't been a bad black, on the contrary. First the Spaniards and later many Cubans of Hispanic descent might have concluded that the Havana-born free black carpenter who planned the 1812 slave uprising didn't set the best example; but, for the great majority of Cubans of African descent, Aponte has always been a symbol of resistance and heroism. This I learnt from Sabue, who in turn learnt it from her mother. Trying to make sure I got the message, Sabue, the only great-grandmother I knew alive, talked to me about Aponte as if she'd actually known him: 'Aponte was a handsome *nengre* [black], loved and as handsome as they come', and a man of great exploits.

When Sabue finally tired of life, I was all night at her wake, where the drums never stopped in her palm thatch hut down in the bush. I wasn't afraid to accompany her to the cemetery. I really felt her death.

Like my maternal grandmother Alberta, my other grandmother on my father's side, who everyone revered with the grand name of Mama, had fourteen children, but in inverse gender: four females and ten males. One of them was my father. My grandfather died before I was born, but Mama had also been born free in the last quarter of the nineteenth century and was of Yoruban descent.

---

4

A woman of Gangá, group of the Bantu nation origins.

The memories of our grandparents and great-grandparents were filled with stories recreated between reality and imagination, which became one and the same. Time and distance didn't seem beyond reach, but, on the contrary, were brought closer by Mama who always had another story to tell of black generals in the wars of independence against Spain and her collaboration in the Mambís[5] insurrection.

I didn't go around boasting my two grandmothers had been born free in the last quarter of the nineteenth century, but I felt very proud of them, for all they had inculcated in me. One way or another, this has kept me, and my children, going to confront, wherever it surfaces, the bitter legacy of slavery which is the racism that has prevailed throughout the twentieth century, and is unending.

Slavery lasted three hundred and sixty years in Cuba. Between 1526 and 1886, over a million Africans of different ethnic groups were transported across the Atlantic to work in the mines, the sugar plantations, coffee, tobacco, domestic service, and the construction of housing and forts. They were only able to bring with them their cultures and their religious beliefs, some instruments they reproduced in the new lands, and the power of memory which remains to this day.

That's why, on my first visit to Africa, in early December 1998, my thoughts were inevitably with my *viejas*.[6] Together with men and women from 27 countries of the Americas, Europe and Africa, I was taking part in a colloquium of Afro-Ibero-American studies in Grand Bassam, close to Abidjan, capital of the Ivory Coast – only a few hours' journey from Elmina Castle in Ghana, one of the infamous slaving port-cities on the coast of West Africa.

Whether by chance I don't know, but on the hot, clear afternoon of December 4, a group of us were at the beach. I walked alone for a while on the terra cotta-coloured sand, like that of Cuba's Caribbean beaches. There was only one thing I could think about on such an occasion. I tried to imagine the suffering of the crossing, the capture and the complicity of Africans on the continent who went along with the European slavers trading in human cargo – one of the themes of the symposium – and reflect on the extent to which the legacy of slavery linked to colonialism and neocolonialism continued to weigh on Africans in their own lands as well as on all of us in the African diaspora.

The date was special, for me and the others from Cuba. Back on our Caribbean island, it was the

---

5
*Mambí* was the African-derived term used for the independence fighters.

6
*Viejas*, which literally translated as 'old ladies', is used as a term of endearment.

day when thousands of drum rituals celebrated *Changó*, an important *orisha* or divinity in the Yoruba pantheon, and the name by which one of the most popular religions of African origin continues in Cuba, also known as *Regla de Ocha* or *Santería*.

The African cultural heritage has been preserved on the island up until this day thanks to the oral tradition passed down to us by those Afro-Cuban gatekeepers who have been our parents, grandparents and great-grandparents; rituals are the communicating vessels with our origins.

Despite this, until recently there had been no monument to commemorate slavery, until the recent totemic sculpture of Alberto Lescay in the hills surrounding El Cobre, near Santiago de Cuba. (See page VI, VII). There have been, in different periods of the twentieth century, sculptures, museums and monuments that have been allegoric, including the many sculptures dedicated to Major General Antonio Maceo y Grajales, the man who symbolizes and synthesizes the rebellion of all Cubans because, among other things, in 1878 he rejected the truce proposed by Spain for a negotiated end to the Ten Years' War, as Spain refused to include the abolition of slavery in the talks.

One of the sculptures erected to the memory of the Bronze Titan (as Maceo, a great mulatto warrior and man of great ideals, was also called) is in Cacahual, on the outskirts of Havana, the country's capital. Another is in the park that bears his name on the Havana seafront, where he is riding horseback facing the centre of the island, not north. Busts and statues have gone up to his mother, Mariana Grajales, who from the early twentieth century has been considered the mother of the nation. The most outstanding of these is in the eastern town of Guantánamo.

In the early 1990s, a sculpture of Maceo was unveiled in Revolution Square in his birth city Santiago de Cuba, which was the most allegorical of its time. The work of black Cuban sculptor Alberto Lescay, it represented the most impressive mausoleum to be put up in Cuba since the 1959 Revolution. The warrior figure of Maceo, also on horseback, can be seen from all angles surrounded by 23 huge structures rising to the sky which represent machetes – the feared tool-turned-weapon used by Cuban Creoles and freed blacks when they rose up in arms on 10 October 1868. That day, planter Carlos Manuel de Céspedes set an example to his class and liberated the slaves on his La Demajagua plantation. With the cry of independence from Spanish rule and the involvement of blacks in that struggle, a nation was in the making. Patriotic homage to a legendary national hero, the sculpture, according to Lescay, also carries within it a strong redemption.

Maceo was born into a Santiago de Cuba free coloured family in 1845. My grandmother Mama, who was particularly fascinated by his imposing figure, told me that when Maceo was little there were times he'd be seen talking to slaves in the slave depot close to his home. There he first heard the word freedom. When he was 23, he joined the struggle for Cuba's independence; in 1896, he died fighting, as did his father Marcos Maceo and his brothers before him.

Despite the fact that the slave trade was officially abolished in Cuba in 1865, the clandestine trade continued and slavery was not abolished until 1886. In 1873, during the war, what is thought to have been the last cargo of African slaves arrived in Cuba. Amongst them were possibly some of my own ancestors.

Like my two grandfathers, many soldiers and officers in the first war of independence were black. When the veterans tried to resuscitate the independence movement in the 1879-80 Little War, the colonial press led a virulent campaign painting the patriotic struggle as a race uprising. But they were struggling for a republic 'with all and for the good of all', as in the rallying call of José Martí, a Cuban of Spanish origin who, in exile in the United States at the end of the nineteenth century, founded the Cuban Revolutionary Party. Martí fell in battle in 1895, in his first and last attempt to turn his words of redemption into deeds. With the fall of Maceo a year later, the aspirations of those who envisioned a united Cuba for all Cubans were frustrated as the United States entered the war and negotiated a treaty with Spain, without Cuba.

And so, it was not until a few years ago, 1997 to be exact, that Cuba commemorated specifically the slave past, in the form of the Monument to the Runaway Slave. Part of UNESCO's international project on the route of the slave, there will also be a museum dedicated to slavery and the copper mines, considered to be the oldest in the Americas. The town, Santiago del Prado de El Cobre, took its name from *el cobre*, the copper, discovered by the Spaniards in the sixteenth century. The monument took a year of intense labour to complete. The idea was that of sculptor Alberto Lescay and the director of *Casa del Caribe* in Santiago de Cuba, Joel James. Lescay describes the piece as a 'song to the spirituality of the hills charged with the energy of men and women who sweated and toiled over the centuries, working the land for its metal…'

In addition to geographical, cultural and spiritual considerations, one of the key motivating factors in selecting the spot was historical. Between 1731 and 1800, slaves working the mines successively took on Spanish troops until finally they defeated them, forcing the king of Spain to concede their freedom. This has gone down in history as the first victorious slave rebellion in the Caribbean, which makes it important on the slave route.

The vertical bronze figure, forged in workshops of the Caguayo Foundation, which Lescay heads, is just over nine meters high. It is set in an iron piece, which is one of the huge pots used for boiling the sugar juice taken from a nineteenth-century sugar mill. The pot symbolizes the 'Nganga', the receptacle for the attributes of the spirits in the Afro-Cuban religion of Congo, called *Regla de Palo*, or *Palo Monte*, originating in Angola.

For many Cubans, however, the most colossal monument against slavery has been the blood shed by Cubans on successive internationalist missions against colonialism, starting in the Congo in 1965. Ten years later, Cuba's military involvement in Angola became a southern African epic, a fitting contribution to the overthrow of apartheid in South Africa by the sons and daughters of a people whose veins flow with African blood. Such sentiments were to be found in the words of Cuban President Fidel Castro in 1976 when he said: 'Those who one day captured and sent slaves to the Americas, perhaps could never have imagined that one of those peoples to have received slaves would send its combatants to fight for the freedom of Africa.'

To this day, Cuba has no museum on slavery and slave trade such as those in the English cities of Hull and Liverpool. The first bears the name of Hull's illustrious British abolitionist William Wilberforce. The second is the Maritime Museum of the Slave Trade in Liverpool, one of the two great British slave ports. Bristol is the other, but it has no equivalent museum dedicated to its slave trading past.

Though there are statues in the Caribbean to the memory of the region's maroons, or runaway slaves, I do not believe any one to be eloquently symbolic enough to reflect the atrocities and legacy of that triangular trade between Africa, Europe and the Americas. The media of today all too frequently remind us that the scourge of slavery continues through Africa, wracked by ethnic civil wars, famines, epidemics, forced displacement, endemic racism, economic hyper-dependence, systematic over-exploitation of its natural resources, political corruption and countless other calamities tending towards the mass extinction of its people.

A simple monument could be an initiative on the part of countries that, in one form or another, took part in the triangular trade to provide systematic aid to the African continent to eradicate at least some of that legacy.

In January 2001, the University of Havana conferred an Honorary Doctorate on Nigerian writer of Yoruba origin, Wole Soyinka, winner of the Nobel Prize for Literature in 1986 (coincidentally the year marking the centenary of the abolition of slavery in Cuba). Soyinka spoke of the ties of friendship between Cubans and Africans and declared that the many young Africans studying in Cuba carried with them a seal of development and success. He referred to Cuba's aid to Africa in the struggle against colonialism, followed by an army of teachers and doctors helping develop the region – all of which Nelson Mandela had singled out on multiple occasions.

What better monument than that?

At the start of the twenty-first century, with galloping globalization, such a gesture should be neither a pipe dream nor difficult to undertake. If a poor, small country like Cuba could build its own solidarity with Africa in the form of free scholarships for thousands of students from Africa and other parts of the so-called Third World, it should not be too much to ask of the rich nations in question an altruistic gesture of this nature. In the final analysis, many of their economies were grounded on slave labour and the fruits of colonialism. At the same time, each and every country in Europe and the Americas which benefited from or suffered the consequences of the slave trade and slavery should also have at least a modest mausoleum as a lasting testimony. Africa records its role in the triangular trade with two historic sites: Elmina, in Ghana, and Gorée island, two miles outside Dakar, capital of Senegal. A place of pilgrimage for Africans of the diaspora and declared UNESCO World Patrimony, the isle preserves the trace of that terrible past, including the gate of no return through which the human cargo passed for export to the New World.

Erecting monuments recording the facts would not be designed to inflict greater wounds on human memory but rather cleanse them so that they can heal one day. In the final analysis, it is about paying a debt. Others have been paid. This one remains.

Translation Jean Stubbs

# Lowell Fiet

## Puerto Rico, Slavery, Race: Faded Memories, Erased Histories

A plaque on a marble wall of the north wing of Puerto Rico's Capitol in San Juan reads: *22 marzo 1873. Quedó abolida la esclavitud en Puerto Rico* (March 22, 1873. Slavery was abolished in Puerto Rico). March 22 is also an official Puerto Rican holiday, *El Día de la Abolición de la Esclavitud* (Abolition of Slavery Day): schools, government offices and banks close for the entire day; stores and other commercial concerns remain open until noon or 1:00 p.m. Like most other Puerto Rican 'national' holidays, 'Abolition Day' is more taken for granted than observed through celebratory or ceremonial acts.

By contrast, Puerto Rico's factual record of the enslavement of indigenous and imported labourers, and of the transatlantic slave trade in general, is one of the longest in the history of the Americas. The enslavement of Taínos (Arawaks) began shortly after Columbus first visited the island in 1493. By 1509 slaves of African origin had accompanied their Spanish holders to Puerto Rico and shipments of enslaved labourers from Africa date from 1519. The African slave population grew rapidly throughout the sixteenth century and the importation of new slaves continued until the mid-nineteenth century. The declaration in 1873 by the then liberal Spanish National Assembly to 'forever' abolish slavery in Puerto Rico liberated the estimated 30,000 black and mulatto slaves still being held and began to close – freedom was gradual and not immediate – the 380-year history of enslavement and oppression.

In spite of the extensive documentation and the rather long period of almost one hundred and thirty years since abolition, issues of race, slavery and African cultural heritage still arouse varying degrees of discomfort and ambivalence. These feelings can be characterized by three interrelated attitudes. The first is a 'the less said the better' notion that positions all questions about race and slavery in the nostalgic context of national folklore. The second assumes the saying *el que no tiene dinga, tiene mandinga* (everybody has a bit of African blood somewhere) which appears regularly, as it does here in the Fortunato Vizcarrondo poem *¿Y tu agüela, a'onde ejtá?* (show me your grandmother before you call me black), to reflect the widely accepted but problematic construction of a tripartite Puerto Rican national racial identity based on the admixture of Spanish, Taíno and African genetic traits. The third attitude asserts that although Puerto Rico, like much of the rest of the Caribbean, suffers from negrophobia and functions as a social, economic and cultural 'pigmentocracy', it is not a racist society in the same way or to the same degree as the United States. In each of these cases, and there are many possible variations, the overriding argument seems to recommend that slavery is better forgotten than remembered, better portrayed as colourful and exotic folklore than examined as social history, and better viewed as unrelated to contemporary everyday life and to such hard-edged problems as rigid economic and social divisions, unemployment, high crime rates, drug trafficking, AIDS, teenage pregnancies, domestic violence, and so forth, than explored for possible responses to the same social dilemmas.

These attitudes also explain the controversy stirred up in 1980 by the publication of the essay *El país de cuatro pisos* (the four-floored country) by José Luis González. González's basic premise questioned the ingredients of Puerto Rican national and cultural identity:

> 'It is now commonplace to say that this [Puerto Rican popular] culture has three historical roots: the Taíno, the African, and the Spanish. What is not commonplace, and in fact, the contrary, is to affirm that of these three roots, the most important, for economic and social reasons, and in cultural consequences, is the African.'

From a brief (and contested) review of the first three centuries of Spanish colonization, González draws the following conclusions:

> 'Puerto Rican popular culture, essentially Afro-Caribbean in character, made us, during the first three centuries of our post-Columbian history, another Caribbean society … If Puerto Rican society would have evolved from then on in the same form as other Caribbean islands, our current 'national culture' would be popular, mestizo, and primordially Afro-Caribbean.'

However, that course changed radically at the beginning of the nineteenth century with waves of European immigrants, the revitalization of sugar plantations on the island, and the arrival of increased numbers of African slaves. Relatively ignored for more than two centuries, Puerto Rico suddenly assumed major importance to the foundering Spanish empire of the nineteenth century. By 1898, González's pre-1800 Puerto Rico, 'another [Afro-]Caribbean society', had become, in demographic terms at least, Europeanized.

Puerto Rico's rapid social and economic development in the nineteenth century – the laying of González's second floor – tends to obscure the first three centuries of Spanish colonial domination. Free and enslaved Africans resided on the Iberian Peninsula before the time of Columbus' voyages to the New World. The presence of free blacks in Puerto Rico is recorded as early as 1495, and a relatively large free black and mulatto population characterizes the island's social development throughout the period of slavery and Spanish colonial control. As stated above, by 1509, *ladino* (Spanish-speaking) African slaves accompanied their Spanish owners to Puerto Rico, and early documentation reveals an uprising in 1514 among *ladino* slaves which led to the request that slaves be shipped directly from Africa to Puerto Rico. The first ship carrying African *bozales* (speakers of African languages) to replace the depleted work force of indigenous peoples arrived in 1519. By 1530, the 'de Lando census' shows that Africans constituted roughly sixty per cent of the island population. The decimation of the indigenous population – the result of sickness, overwork, armed resistance, flight and suicide – required increasing numbers of Africans to mine for gold, and after the exhaustion of the mines, to plant, harvest and process sugar cane. At the same time, because of the severe imbalance, there being a far greater number of African men than women, African men and indigenous women cohabited – as did Spanish men and indigenous women – with the probable result of a strong Afro-Amerindian racial and cultural admixture at the beginning of the colonial process.

    The rich cultural history of enslaved and free Africans and their descendants over the past five hundred years includes their diverse origins in over thirty ethnic groups from varied regions that cover much of the African continent, numerous uprisings and rebellions, the establishment of free black and mulatto communities, the emergence of major figures in art, education and politics, such as the painter José Campeche (1751-1809), the teacher Rafael Cordero (1790-1868) and the medical doctor and politician Dr. José Celso Barbosa (1857-1921), as well as those of mixed ancestry, such as the radical separatist Dr. Ramón Emeterio Betances (1827-1899) and the nationalist leader Pedro Albizu Campos (1891-1965). Also unique forms of creative expression, religious worship and community organization emerged – which continue to be reflected in present-day Puerto Rican society. The military role played by blacks and mulattos in the rejection of the 1797 British invasion by General Ralph Abercromby at the head of 6,000 troops pays particular tribute to the cultural resilience and social ingenuity of the Afro-Puerto Rican population. These factors all lend support to José Luis González's idea of the importance of the African heritage to the development of Puerto Rico's popular culture.

In the last years, University of Puerto Rico professors, artists and intellectuals have attempted to redress the academic apathy surrounding Abolition Day, as well as the generalized ambivalence about issues related to race, through the organization of a series of lectures and exhibits. Writer Mayra Santos Febres plays a crucial role as the *provocatrice* of this effort; other contributing figures include Isabelo Zenón, author of *Narciso descubre su trasero* (Narcissus discovers his behind), an important study on racism and culture in Puerto Rico, sociologist Manuel Febres, literary scholar and dancer Marie Ramos, historian Juan Giusti, social researcher Palmira Ríos of the University's Institute of Caribbean Studies and curator and scholar Héctor Bermúdez Zenón. The Museum of the Black Puerto Rican Man and Woman in the city of Humacao, on Puerto Rico's East Coast, inaugurated under Bermúdez Zenón's direction in 1996, serves as an example of a renewed interest in celebrating March 22.

Prior efforts should also be noted. Since the 1973 centennial of abolition, the Institute of Puerto Rican Culture and other public and privately funded agencies have supported impressive art and historical exhibits, commemorative posters, research projects, and documentary films on Puerto Rico's Afro-Caribbean heritage. The pictorial/photo essay on nineteenth-century slave rebellions, *El machete de Ogún* (1990) (Ogun's cutlass) compiled by, among others, historian Guillermo Baralt, writers Lydia Milagros González and Ana Lydia Vega, and the documentary film *La tercera raíz* (1994) (The third root), based on the 1992 quincentenary exhibit of the same title, written by Lydia Milagros González and directed by Carlos Malavé, exemplify efforts that combine museum, archival, and social research and disseminate information about slavery and Puerto Rico's Afro-Caribbean heritage in convincing and accessible formats.

Other commemorative artifacts, such as the statue in Cabo Rojo of Ramón Emeterio Betances, who was Puerto Rico's strongest voice supporting abolition, can also be construed as a tribute to the end of slavery in Puerto Rico. Similarly, the statue in Bayamón of José Celso Barbosa, the famed black Puerto Rican autonomist and later statehood advocate, serves as testimony to the accomplishments of Afro-Puerto Ricans. Yet, beyond the Capitol's plaque and the March 22 holiday, the only other State-sanctioned symbol or monument that specifically focuses on the abolition of slavery and commemorates the lives of enslaved Africans during the 380-year history of slavery in Puerto Rico, is an often overlooked statue of a black man with broken chains erected in the 1960s in Abolition park in the city of Ponce on the south coast.

The value of officially-sanctioned artifacts and symbols, whether monuments, statues, busts, plaques or national holidays, is unquestionable. There should be stronger symbolic representation of the African presence in Puerto Rican history and culture, yet symbols, in and of themselves, are rarely enough to sustain historical memory. The tendency in Puerto Rico has been to minimize as opposed to recognize and reinforce the contributions of Afro-Puerto Ricans, both before and after the 1873 abolition of slavery. Without more rigorous curricular support from public and private education institutions and a greater response from local cultural organizations, the signifying force of a monument, statue or other symbol commemorating abolition or the lives and culture of enslaved and free Puerto Ricans of African descent, would continue to fade from memory, or worse, merely justify historical omission.

A number of texts are essential to addressing the themes of race, slavery and African cultural heritage in Puerto Rico. These include the following:

Alvarez Nazario, Manuel, *El elemento afronegroide en el español de Puerto Rico* (San Juan, Puerto Rico: Instituto de Cultura Puertorriqueña 1974).

Baralt, Guillermo A., *Esclavos rebeldes: conspiraciones y sublevaciones de esclavos en Puerto Rico* (1795-1873) (Río Piedras, Puerto Rico: Ediciones Huracán 1982).

Baralt, Guillermo A. (et al.), *El machete de Ogún: Las luchas de los esclavos en Puerto Rico* (Río Piedras, Puerto Rico: CEREP, Proyecto de Divulgación Popular 1989).

Díaz Soler, Luis, *Historia de la esclavitud negra en Puerto Rico* (1493-1890) [1953], 2nd ed. (Río Piedras, Puerto Rico: Editorial de la Universidad de Puerto Rico 1965).

González, José Luis, *El país de cuatro pisos y otros ensayos* (Río Piedras, Puerto Rico: Ediciones Huracán 1980).

Picó, Fernando, *Historia general de Puerto Rico* (Río Piedras, Puerto Rico: Ediciones Huracán 1986).

Scarano, Francisco A., *Puerto Rico: Cinco siglos de historia* (San Juan, Puerto Rico [and elsewhere]: McGraw-Hill 1993).

Sued Badillo, Jalil and Angel López Cantos, *Puerto Rico Negro* (Río Piedras, Puerto Rico: Editorial Cultural 1986).

Zenón, Isabelo, *Narciso descubre su trasero: El negro en la cultura Puertorriqueña*, 2 vols., 2nd ed. (Humacao, Puerto Rico: Editorial Furidi 1975).

Flávio dos Santos Gomes

# The Legacy of Slavery and Social Relations in Brazil

On the 13th of May 1888, Brazil became the last country in the Americas to abolish the slavery of blacks. As late as the last decades of the nineteenth century, authorities, landlords, politicians, scientists and members of parliament were still discussing the abolition of slavery and the fate of the freedmen. Many believed and defended the notion that slavery could survive until the early decades of the twentieth century. Abolitionists and emancipators, however, would affirm that progress and civilization could only be achieved in Brazil after the abolition of slavery. They also discussed the need to create a market of free labour, but by free labour they usually meant European immigrants. Some leading authorities in the fields of sciences and letters would argue – with a degree of pessimism – that the destiny of the young nation would be damaged by the intensive miscegenation between whites and blacks, and that the outcome would be a degenerate race. To others, this very interbreeding meant salvation. The continual miscegenation of blacks and their descendants would lead to more whites, who could be regarded as 'civilized citizens'.

One hundred and ten years after abolition, Brazil now has a black population (classified as mulattos and blacks by the *Instituto Brasileiro de Geografia e Estatística*) of almost seventy million people. It is the second largest black population in the world, after Nigeria. Despite this fact, the black population in Brazil is almost invisible. Generally speaking, blacks are barely represented in parliament, in the established circles of power or in the universities. Even on television and in advertisements, black men and women are invisible. In the socioeconomic indicators, the black population always manifests unequivocal and repetitive inequality.

In 1988, during the celebrations of the centenary of abolition, two public events reflecting on the past took place. One of them was conducted by the academic world – always with institutional support – with publications, seminars and congresses, many of them international. They sought to analyse the manner in which slavery and its abolition took place in Brazil. The purpose of these events was to denote a slavery past which was at the same time both heterogeneous and very distant. The past was recalled to mark its distance in time. Yet, what about the changes and transformations for the population of African descent? Were there any? This was the question posed by the organizations that fight against racial discrimination in Brazil. Through public events, lectures, concerts and an important march that gathered millions of people in the centre of Rio de Janeiro, there was a profound reflection and, for the most part, denunciation of the conditions of sociracial inequality in the year of the centenary of abolition.

In 1995, the black social movements began to resume their action. At this time, they were celebrating the third centenary of the death of Zumbi dos Palmares (November 20, 1695), the most celebrated leader of the primary *quilombo* (maroon enclave) de Palmares, in the northeast of colonial Brazil. The dates of the celebrations would be used as a symbol of the struggle and the denunciation of racial discrimination and the social conditions of blacks, in other words, their lack of full citizenship and human rights. The 13th of May, more than abolition itself, would represent a continuation of the process by which the black population found itself excluded. On the other hand, the 20th of November would stand for the continuation of the struggle and the resistance to oppression.

Does slavery explain racism? Do circumstances and reproduction of socioeconomic disadvantages faced by the population of African descent in Brazil nowadays have their historical origins in the establishment of a society based on slavery? Old interpretations and renewed debates. These arguments were used on numerous occasions by scholars who looked at slavery and race relations in Brazil. They worked in an atmosphere of a wide-ranging intellectual debate – which influenced even the comparative works that dealt with the issue of slavery in Brazil and in the United States.

The 'historical roots' that relate slavery to racism were conceived during the establishment of racial typologies and ideologies. From the end of the nineteenth century until the Second World War, Brazilian intellectuals analysed the racial problems in Brazil under the perspective of a *social Darwinism* and therefore emphasized, most of the time, the 'trauma' of slavery. It was in this scientific and ideological context that they searched for a specific interpretation of the past of slavery and the relations between whites and blacks in Brazil.

The understanding of the establishment of the slave-based societies in the Americas, as well as the manner in which they were destroyed, has always been the concern of anthropologists, historians and sociologists. They all tried to justify the pattern of contemporary race relations. The past was evoked to explain the present and, sometimes, even the future. They went in search of myths to explain the origins. What were the similarities and the differences between the slave societies of Brazil, the United States, Cuba and the various Caribbean islands? Which social and economic aspects determined the existing systems of racial relations in these areas?

Slavery and Social Thought in Brazil

In Brazil, a new emphasis in this field of concern could be seen in the work of Gilberto Freyre (1933).[1] In later studies, the fundamental crux of the debate was to determine if slavery had been good or bad, judged according to aspects of *violence, dehumanization, patriarchy* and *paternalism* in the relations between masters and slaves. Generally speaking, Freyre defended the notion of *benevolence* of the Brazilian slave system. His interpretations, from an anthropological point of view, were to regain their authority, as their influences were extended to studies on slavery in the United States. In general, there was an attempt to systematize the explanations for the origin of those aspects seen as 'benevolent' in the Brazilian slave system in contrast to those perceived as 'malevolent' in the North American system. At that time, these reflections were to establish the basis for the interpretation of the race relations systems in these two countries. Harmony and conflicts would have had their historical origins here.

In the forties and fifties, many other scholars went on to study the issues of slavery and race relations. The focus on the comparative perspective continued to be preferred. Still concerned with the differences and similarities, many authors tried to explain the historical process of what they understood as racial tensions in Brazil. The main theses were subjected to revision. Under this perspective, the early 1960s studies of Davis, Boxer and Harris stood out. Instead of stressing the differences, they started to demonstrate – through specific cases – the similarities between the slave systems in the Americas. In the beginning of the fifties, when UNESCO proposed comprehensive research on racial relations in Latin America, many regional studies appeared in Brazil, particularly from Brazilian sociologists and anthropologists.

The historiographical studies from the sixties led to wholesale revisions. These contested the previous interpretations that classified slavery in Brazil as 'mild'. In the context of these revisions, the approaches to the forms of slave resistance, especially collective expressions, had pride of place. The objective of these critical interpretations was not to mystify the assumed notions which emphasized the passivity and the submission of the slaves in Brazil. Contrary to previous interpretations, slavery was described as a cruel and violent regime. The conditions which determined its existence would be, among other things, the dehumanization of the captives

---

[1] Gilberto Freyre, *Casa-grande & sensala: Formaçao da familia brasileira sob o regimen de economia patriarchal* (Río de Janeiro: Schmidt 1933).

and therefore, the various social processes experienced by them. Besides, the analyses of some of these revisionist authors emphasized the acts of rebellion of the slaves. In this way, slave resistance was stressed as a mere factor that determined the reactions of captives to the violence imposed by their masters and the conditions in which they lived and worked.

By focusing on the studies that emphasized the analysis of slave rebellion in Brazil, this historiographical school of revision went to the other extreme of the previous reflections, most of which were based on the arguments of Gilberto Freyre, which accentuated the 'benevolent' aspect of the slave system in Brazil. Here, slave resistance is represented in a romantic form. The passive and submissive slaves of previous interpretations were now described performing acts of heroism and admirable courage. If in the mild slave system, where the landlord was seen as a friend, the slave was depicted as submissive, in a violent system, characterized by cruel masters, the captives were seen as rebels. In this way, the explanatory binomials are replaced. These studies also pointed out the total absence of approaches that tried to analyse the attitudes and actions of the slaves as agents of historical transformations during slavery. The slaves were ascribed roles as mute actors during the passage of history. In these analyses, which were fundamentally based on assumed theories which have crystallized over time, the explanation of the slave society in Brazil and its complexity was based on the verification of its violent character and the practices of social control exercised by the dominant classes. Therefore, the acts of confrontation by the captives were reduced to a simple 'reaction' to the cruel and violent regime which kept them in captivity. In the face of an oppressive system that regarded the captives as mere merchandise, reflections about the values, objectives and various interpretations of slave life and culture were seen as totally trivial. There were other significant approaches to slave culture. The topic of black protest was also highlighted.

Although this historiographical tendency has its theoretical, empirical and, most of all, political relevance in the criticism of assumed notions which characterized the benevolence of slave society in Brazil, it persisted in using instruments of analysis which dehumanized slaves in the social world. Because he was not considered as an historical subject, in these analyses the slave was portrayed as a warrior, whose actions seemed to be oriented by an inexorable logic with a sole historical purpose. In other words, the passive thing/slave left the scene and was replaced by the rebel thing/slave. Therefore, the myth of the Brazilian slave was inverted.

Trying to differentiate between some of the essential aspects in these opposing analyses, more recent studies – with new approaches – have significantly broadened the horizon for reflections upon the social history of slavery in Brazil. Among the topics that stand out in these more recent approaches of Brazilian historiography, we can mention paternalism, social control and mobilizations by part of the slaves in the everyday notions of slavery, black culture, slave rebellions and resistance, slave families, racism among whites, slaves and blacks at the end of the nineteenth century, the emancipation and traffic of slaves.

There has been a renovation, not only thematic but also methodological and theoretical, in the historiography of Brazilian slavery. There has been an attempt to analyse the various cultural, religious and social dimensions, and the historical meanings of slavery and freedom. The economic and sociodemographic aspects, supposedly inexorable and crystallized, became relative. Generalizing sociological reflections and/or economic approaches gave way to the analyses of social history and culture. There has also been a concern to identify the perspective of *Time and Space* in these more recent historiographical revisions. With its agents and subjects, slavery in Brazil was not an historical experience with a single scenario and a linear perspective. To rediscover scenarios and their contexts meant to evaluate different scripts and characters, with multiple faces and complex manifestations. From a critical point of view, the images of slavery in Brazil – instead of being distorted and blurred – gained a new focus and appearance. They contemplated not only the masters, punishments and violence, but also the captives and their cultural, communal and family reinventions. A linear history of slavery that had been transformed in the sixties, seventies and the beginning of the eighties into a history of the *slave system*, would in the nineties gain the appearance of a history of the black experience in Brazil.

Bringing new analyses and approaches to the discussion, the universe of the historiographical debate was expanded with these studies. For instance, slave resistance was understood in a broader social context of complex struggles, with multi-faceted aspects, which were invented by the slaves in their everyday lives. Also, the forms of confrontation and mobilization exercised by the captives began to be viewed as something that, among other things, had as a counterpoint the continuous creation of new relations with their masters. In these relations, the forms of domination and social control were modified through subtle, invisible and permanent oppositions. As they expanded the combined body of reflection on the slaves, these new studies tried to perceive an organization of slave labour, the constitution of families, the kinship and intimacy of spiritual ties, cultural and religious practices etc., in an effort to recreate part of the historical experiences of the slaves. Ultimately, they tried to invoke the life experiences of the slaves, and therefore, the slaves as agents of transformation in the slave societies, salvaging through their historical behaviour, actions and appeals for independence and the birth of an autonomous slave community with its own culture and political logic. In brief, what these more recent studies pointed out, in general terms, was that the captives resorted to original strategies of survival, protest and confrontation against the policies of master domination, thereby inventing a slave community with its own logic.

### History and Struggle against Racism

It would be interesting to connect the analyses of academic studies on slavery and racial relations in Brazil with the uprising mobilization of the black community. When and how do black intellectuals adopt various themes in the history of slavery – especially the *quilombos*, rebellions and religiosity – as a political expression of the struggle against racial discrimination and the desire to create esteem for the 'black culture'? Certainly, it was not only at the end of the seventies, with the appearance of the MNU (Unified Black Movement). These themes could already be perceived in the so called 'black press' in the twenties in São Paulo. But it was at the end of the seventies that new forms of political construction and reworkings of the idea of black protest against slavery became explicit.

For the black social movements – at least those emerging in the seventies – black resistance also appeared to be a symbol which required careful handling. Many of the labels of black protests (struggling heroes, cultural resistance, etc.) were 'reinvoked' to create an ethnic identity. The *quilombos* for example, especially Palmares – were at the same time synonymous with struggle and direct and armed conflict. They also represented the realm of ideas (as a socially constructed space) for cultural resistance. An appropriate tool was found to fight against racial discrimination. How? By creating an identity for black people. Let us remember that at this stage, the *quilombismo* of Abdias Nascimento existed. No doubt, it was a perspective to analyze Brazil with 'pan-African' eyes. It was, ideally, in the *quilombo* that the Brazilian negros united their forces. Their resistance against racism had its 'historical origin' in the *quilombos*. The meanings constructed around the *quilombos* were also the key to the perception of the blacks as political subjects of a certain 'history of the oppressed' from the seventies on.

It is possible to make the following speculation: to what extent were the approaches of historians, anthropologists and sociologists to the black rebellion – particularly those dedicated to the *mocambos* (slave enclaves in the forest) – marked by a perspective of harmony versus racial conflict? Palmares, for example, the most important symbol of black resistance in Brazil, was described (and this discourse has been reproduced by several intellectuals) as a permissive society for blacks and Indians. It was, therefore, devoid of racial intolerance. Finally, the discourse about black ethnology in Brazil was partially constructed using the *quilombos* as a paradigm. Beyond ethnology, it was a paradigm of culture and race. It is essential to reflect on how history was 'read', or if you prefer 'recovered', to generate various logical and inexorable representations of the slave period. Memories, omissions, approximations, remoteness, violence, benevolence, harmony and conflicts would be the scripts for the various historical reconstructions that were possible. Between memory and legacy, slavery (and the historical experiences of its subjects) was a past that should remain in a very distant time.

Although invisible to some, there was an implicit dialogue between the more contemporary historiographical production about slavery in Brazil and black social movements. The reflections (inside and outside the academic world) on social relations and socioeconomic inequalities in Brazil were essential, in a sense that they generated further considerations about an historical past from which there were sometimes attempts to approximate, sometimes to distance. With antagonistic perspectives, many social sectors tried to establish a relationship between slavery and racism. With an homogenizing discourse of a nation and the more universalist one of an ethnic identity, Brazilian society was interpreted by intellectual sectors and public authorities as being devoid of racism. Many pointed to the existence of inequalities and differences. But they also talked about interbreeding and the legacy of slavery. The *Africans* would have been transformed into slaves. They were the blacks. And now they would all be Brazilians. According to these analyses, more inequality was to be found between the rich and the poor than between *blacks* and whites. This eliminated difference in and from history.

From another perspective, black racial movements would reinforce the dialogue of ethnic identity. More than individual and/or relational, racial inequalities would be at the crux of the current debate about the construction of citizenship in Brazil. The complexity of the system of racial classifications would not limit explanations about the forms of creation and recreation of racism. Not *everyone* could classify themselves as being 'white' or 'black'. But *almost everyone* could be classified that way. The social and economic indicators would leave no doubt about the scripts, meanings and colours of inequality. Also, black movements (with their various forms of organization) demanded new roles and representations in history; in contemporary history, in the history of the future and particularly in that of the past, where to be a slave was to be black. Reaffirming identities and denouncing inequalities, historians searched fundamentally for meanings for origins, struggles and cultures. There was an attempt to use history (not only that of the remote past) to explain the differences.

Conclusion

Many of the historical explanations for slavery that have appeared in sociological, anthropological and historical studies – especially between the fifties and the seventies – had one feature in common. They tried to explain slavery by the legacy it had left behind: the inequality and discrimination of the black population. By reflecting on slavery, they tried to show a *transition*. The unaccomplished, stagnated and retrograde world of slavery gave way to a world of modernity, complexity, urbanization and industrialization. These transformations, which were so clear in these analyses, would have provoked contradictions and tensions, especially socioracial ones.

The black would remain the black. In other words, he would continue to be seen as a *victim* in these analyses. Before he was the dehumanized slave of asymmetrical relations, cruelty, violence, promiscuity and social anomia. And afterwards? Afterwards, this slave would become a black, perhaps a citizen from the juridical point of view, but he would not have the same social and economic guarantees. Emphasizing the idea of 'legacy' of slavery, these analyses would try to show the difficulty, perhaps incapacity, of the black to integrate in a new social order, a society of classes and a new world of working relations. From slaves, seen as *victims* of a social system which was finally destroyed, blacks were now almost being blamed for their past and historical origin.

Nevertheless, most of the explanations about the 'legacy' of slavery in the constitution of contemporary racism caused part of history to disappear. The social memory has somehow been erased. And I mean history not as a discipline, method or theory. I argue about the historical process of the post-emancipation period up to the fifties. More than only the realm of ideas of *negative legacy* and *victimization*, it is possible to follow other routes. In this case those of public policies, available scientific frameworks, ideas of nationalism and especially of social struggles, to understand the creation and resurrection of social discrimination in Brazil.

Translation Elizabeth Pinheiro

Livio Sansone

## Remembering Slavery from Nearby: Heritage Brazilian Style

The rear part of the building of the Church of *Nossa Senhora do Rosário e de São Benedicto dos Homens Pretos* in the central and busy Uruguayana Street hosts the only Black People's Museum in the city of Rio de Janeiro. That Church is not just any Church. The present one was rebuilt after a devastating fire on the site where slaves and free men of colour had built a beautiful, rich and conspicuous church of their own. Here the meetings were held of the centuries-old Brotherhood with the same name as the Church – though better known as the Brotherhood of Black Men. The *Museu do Negro* was funded, apparently in 1946, by a number of volunteers of the Brotherhood who wanted the black connotation of that specific Church to be remembered. No entrance fee is asked, no professional curator is involved and the exhibit is, to say the least, eclectic. With hardly any written explanation or apparent logical layout, the following array of objects are displayed: images of slaves (most of them engravings by Rugendas and Debret), recent paintings by black artists related to the Brotherhood, torture instruments of all sorts, images of saints (especially St. Benedict, the African saint), maps of Africa and Brazil, a few portraits of princess Isabel (who signed the Act to abolish slavery in 1888), a full-size replica of the tomb of the princess and her husband (in a section called *Galeria Imperial*), portraits of Senghor and Martin Luther King, a series of portraits of marshal Baptista de Matos (a black army officer, head of the Brotherhood, who had sponsored the restoration of the *Museu* after the 1967 fire), a series of portraits of illustrious abolitionists, a large painting of Yemanyá next to a huge gypsum head of a screaming slave and a couple of wood engravings of the slave Anastácia (always represented with a *mordaça*, a gag).

    The collection stirs up sentiments of sufferance, pity and solidarity, but it still evokes a feeling of magic. This feeling, at first, I could not grasp. I inquired with the caretaker and with several people who by the entrance sell candles, *santinhos*, statues of saints and calendars. Nobody was able to tell me anything except that it was, of course, the *Museu do Negro*. I found the explanation for that magical atmosphere in the facial expressions of the surprisingly numerous visitors. Brazilian museums usually attract very few national visitors – though the recent trend of travelling exhibitions of, mostly, European collections has been successful with the urban upper middle class. Here, the visitors came to touch a number of objects, pray and meditate. The small *Museu do Negro* is, in fact, a support act for the main attraction, the worship of the slave Anastácia,[1] which daily brings hundreds, if not thousands of people to visit that church to pay tribute, comply with a religious obligation, light a candle and pray and ask for grace. Most, but not all visitors are black or brown and belong to the lower classes. The power of Anastácia reaches beyond the fussy, but existing colour and class lines. Her sufferance as a muted and mutilated slave is her force as a protector of life today.[2]

In the nearby *Paço Imperial*, the recently restored colonial building where the abolition of slavery was actually declared, modern art galleries are elegantly organized by very competent personnel. Good coffee and snacks can be enjoyed just beside the actual patio where the Act of abolition was signed. No inscription reminds us of that crucial moment – which is rather hilarious since several inscriptions, in nice copper plates, are there to remind us of the councillors and politicians who have sponsored the restoration of that beautiful building. As far as I have noticed, none of the many thousands of passers-by who walk beside the *Paço* on their way to the ferry to Niteroi, inquire about the activities of the cultural centre of the *Paço*. The highly educated, to whom these modern art galleries mainly aim, do not seem uncomfortable with the blatant and continuing act of literally removing cultural memory from the site.

The Afro-Brazilian Museum of Salvador da Bahia, also the only museum of its kind in the city, is another potential site for the organization of memory and heritage surrounding slavery in Brazil. Salvador is as important as Rio in the iconography of the official and popular public representations of Brazil for nationals and foreigners. Moreover, aided by demography, which makes it, after Rio de Janeiro and São Paulo, perhaps the third largest concentration of people of African descent outside Africa,[3] Salvador is the cultural capital of Brazilian *négritude*. The *Museu Afro-Brasileiro* was established by the Federal University of Bahia in 1974, with federal and state

---

[1]
Anastácia, whose real existence has been questioned by many historians, was a slave who was forced to carry an iron mask by her master because her words had inflammatory power on the slaves (see John Burdick, *Blessed Anastacia. Women, Race and Popular Christianity in Brazil* (London: Routledge 1998).

[2]
Recently the Brotherhood appointed a retired museum specialist, herself member of the Brotherhood, as curator. She has the difficult task of running this small museum with no funding as well as keeping out from it the most conspicuous forms of devotion to Anastácia, which are at odds with the policies of the very conservative bishop of Rio.

[3]
According to the 1991 national census, 83% of the almost three million people living in the metropolitan area of Salvador are registered as brown or black.

funding. In contrast to the museum in Rio, it has been part of an ambitious academic project, which however never managed to receive adequate financing. It is harboured in the basement of the prestigious Medical School – from which emerged Nina Rodrigues [4] – and enjoys the dedication of a properly trained curator – with lots of goodwill.

The exhibit is a sophisticated representation of Afro-Bahian culture, or, rather, the way in which a number of key anthropologists who were paradigmatic in the four decades from 1940 to 1980 would have liked Afro-Bahians to be portrayed. The collection consists of a series of artifacts, garments, ornaments and musical instruments relating to the Afro-Brazilian religious system generally called *candomblé*. Some of these 'black objects' are old, others are relatively new. They are accompanied by a series of beautiful pictures by the Bahia-based French ethnographer-photographer Pierre Verger, who was the de facto first curator. In association with each of these Brazilian objects, there is a related object from Africa, more specifically from Dahomey (now Benin), where Verger had been the curator of two museums in Ouidah. The aim of the Bahian exhibit is to suggest – according to the associations that had been developed by Melville Herskovits, Roger Bastide and Pierre Verger – the African origin of Bahian black cultural and religious life. Slavery represents only a very small part of the whole exhibition, and is reduced, once again, to putting on show a couple of instruments of torture or, as they used to say, 'contention'.[5]

[4]
Raimundo Nina Rodrigues (1862-1906) has been considered by many, from Artur Ramos onwards, as the forerunner of modern ethnography on Afro-Brazilian culture and social forms. Nina, though heavily influenced by Lombroso's classification of deviant types and Lamarck's racialization of social deviancy, and considering black cultural forms as basically pathological expressions, indeed sets forth Sílvio Romero's cry for a survival ethnography of the life and culture of Brazilians of African descent – in many ways, identified as the living past of a country striving to enter the future as a 'modern' country.

Praça da Sá, facing the building of the Museu Afro-Brasileiro (Salvador, Bahia).

The exorcism of slavery out of the pantheon of black cultural production is even more signifying if one notices the very site of the museum: right in the heart of the central and ancient neighbourhood called *Pelourinho* – because it contains the square were slaves were whipped and punished in public. The whole area called *Pelourinho* has been renovated over the last decade and has become a major tourist attraction under the name of *Pelô*: both a temple of the Bahian version of *négritude* and regional identity and the site of massive commoditization of things Afro-Brazilian. Young blacks from all over the city flock here to enjoy dancing to live music; tourists from all over the world come here to see young blacks enjoying themselves. The Church built by the slaves, in a similar fashion to the one in Rio and with the same name, and even the Head Quarter of the Brotherhood of Black Men, have become foci of tourist and intellectual curiosity. The rows of beggars outside the Church of St. Francisco also add to this curiosity. They have been there, as it were, without interruption from the period of slavery – beggars were largely, dismissed slaves or the young offspring of slaves.

The cases of Rio and Salvador show that (re)construction of the memory of slavery and its transformation into 'heritage', that is, the preservation of the past for the sake of the future of the nation, has been hampered by a number of obstacles. No attempt has been made to build a monument to slavery, a heritage centre (as we know it in places as different as Gorée and a number of former plantations in the South of the United States) or a museum of slavery.[6] In the sites that

---

[5] The premises of the museum have been recently renovated. In its new exhibits the museum has chosen to leave out from the collection the life-size images of the *orixás* which had contributed to turn the museum into a place of worship – in a 'rationalizing' move which is reminiscent of that of the new curator of the museum in Rio.

Sacred candomblé necklaces and puppets representing *orixás* (Museu Afro-Brasileiro, Salvador Bahia).

have been central in the history of slavery, where a monument to slavery could have belonged, the effort has been directed towards exorcizing the pain of slavery. Even in the celebration of the centenary of the abolition in 1988, when monuments were inaugurated, it always concerned those who had fought slavery: king Zumbi of the Maroon Republic of Palmares was certainly the most popular subject of a series of monuments.[7] Government officials and black activists shared after all a view of what had to be represented and, although having different agendas, had no interest in representing slavery – it embarrassed. No attempt was made to represent in those monuments – often busts – the drama of the plantation society or of slave culture.

There are several reasons for this attitude. Perhaps the main hindrance stems from the relatively short period Brazil has lived without slavery. In 2001 it has only been 111 years. This equates to a quarter of Brazil's modern history – Brazil having become five hundred years old in the year 2000. The scars left by slavery on Brazilian society are still fresh. It can be seen in the present position of colour in social hierarchy, in the difficulties black Brazilians encounter when they venture out of their traditional, submissive place, in the making of survival strategies centred on interracial cordiality and the cultivation of friendship and 'good connections' with important white people. One does not want to solidify memories into monuments when things can still be as they were remembered.

Another major obstacle has been the way Afro-Brazilians have been incorporated into the popular and especially the official representation of the nation: as 'cultural' people, as descendants of Africans who are different from the others because of a number of cultural traits said to be specific to black people. This culturalization of black Brazilians has also been affecting their construction as objects for research: most research has been conducted into black culture and religious life, far less into race relations, racial discrimination and the complex relationship between 'race' and class. In official representations of the nation, slavery has been by and large left to the historians and relegated into the (not so distant) past.

Yet another obstacle to the investment in the politics of recognition based on the enhancement of a notion of heritage is that Brazil, as many other countries in what was once called the Third World, lacks a preservationist attitude. The political society hardly sees any necessity for

6
Only one of the sort is the rather small and ill-equipped *Museu da Abolição* associated to the J. Nabuco Foundation in Recife.
7
Birman, Patricia, 'Maio de 88: outras histórias', *Quase Catalógo*, 6, 1997 (published by the UERJ, State University of Rio de Janeiro).

it; civil society has not yet made heritage part of its political claims. Of course one can easily argue that a country that sees itself as relatively young and progress-orientated (Brazil's national flag is dedicated to Order and Progress) would deal with the Past in ways that are specific and in many ways different from those of the Old World.[8] It could be seen as a waste of money and energy, in a country where historically so little has been invested in the preservation of memory of Afro-Brazilians and their cultural and political production: hardly any specialized libraries and archives exist. Moreover, Brazil's young democracy is recovering from a long period in which the army had a major say and had indeed cultivated monuments and forced society to pay attention to them. This has certainly contributed to the fact that in today's Brazilian cities those monuments, rather than enjoying any attention from passers-by, have become part of the boardwalk cacophony that characterizes city life.

The last obstacle I want to touch upon is formed by the politics of representation of a society in which *metissage* and mixture are not only a demographic and cultural reality, but also part and parcel of the national self-image. Such images of racial and cultural fluidity are tenacious – they are a dream of a better future for the poor and a strategy to prevent claims for 'the haves' – and are paired with the persistence of terrific social rigidity in most domains of life. The relative absence of ethnoracial politics leaves little place for the celebration of past wrongdoings through a monument to slavery.

Interestingly, the only instance in Brazilian society where slavery is consistently remembered is within religion, in particular that of Umbanda – the more syncretic section of the Afro-Brazilian religious system. Umbanda's pantheon contains, in a prominent position, the slave Anastácia, the *Preto Velho* (literally, the Old Black Man) and the *Mãe Preta* (literally, the Black Mother)[9] – three powerful spirits representing different characters among the slaves. As in the catholic tradition, their sufferance is not only the condition for holiness, but also of their power as protectors and healers.

In Brazil the absolute absence of a discussion that would be brought about by any attempt to construct a monument to slavery raises problems. Even though one sees a certain improvement

---

8
See Myrian Santos, 'The Imaginary of the Empire in the Brazilian Museums', Paper delivered at the International Conference, 'Brazil: Representing the Nation'. London: Institute of Latin American Studies, 23-24 November 2000.

over the last years, there is still a backlog of symbolic inclusion of Afro-Brazilians in the official representations of the nation. Public debate on the topic is still almost non-existent. In spite of representing almost half of the population, black Brazilians are penalized by the relative absence of a social pact which institutionalizes moments of negotiation and even (symbolic) reparation for those who have suffered the most. The politics of heritage cannot be seen in abstraction from their social context, in spite of the fact that monuments, such as the one to slavery, are icons that can transmit images that are surprisingly global.

Transatlantic slavery was by definition a transnational phenomenon, which has created a universe of suffering, dehumanization and racialization, spanning across the many regions of what we now know, after Paul Gilroy, as the Black Atlantic – a region that reaches to the tropical lowlands of the Pacific coast of Central and Latin America. Yet, the way in which it is remembered as well as its legacy felt within today's life and race relations, show that the memory of slavery is often a surprisingly 'local', relational and contingent construction.

9
A monument to the *Mãe Preta* was inaugurated in São Paulo in the seventies. Though part of an Umbanda celebration, it has since become an important meeting point for rallies called by black activists.

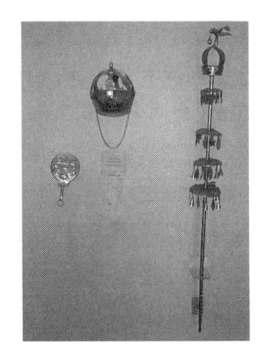

Ornament of a *caboclo* divinity (Museu Afro-Brasileiro, Salvador, Bahia).
Ornament of an *orixá* (Museu Afro-Brasileiro, Salvador, Bahia).

# Hilary Beckles

## Emancipation in the British Caribbean

For some time now scholars on both sides of the Atlantic are in agreement that the legacies of African slavery in western modernity have remained clearly displayed in Caribbean society. The region continues to be torn and tortured by the same contradictory social forces that informed the discourse on slavery. As a consequence, nowhere in the Atlantic world, where societies were shaped by the culture of slavery, are the sentiments surrounding 'emancipation' as both an historic event and a social process, as keenly felt and determining of public policy as they are here.

There is also considerable agreement that Caribbean societies are themselves monuments to freedom and incubators of liberationist political philosophies, enabling working people – both free and enslaved – to live the Enlightenment vision as 'emancipation in action'. In the protracted struggle for freedom, blacks demonstrated a commitment to social idealism that ought to honour them as primary shapers of modernity. Their determination to remove slavery at all cost from the Atlantic world, has made them the leading voice in the emancipation discourse that continues to define and guide Caribbean politics and identity.

Caribbean society then, by virtue of its historical remaking under colonialism, represents a space where the masses have emerged from deepest despair and unimaginable bondage with a culture and mentality that effuse triumphalist celebration. It is a narrative of African ethnic survival against the background of autochthonous genocide that identifies emancipation – both cultural and spiritual – as the overriding sociopsychic postmodern project. For these diasporic African people, this process is perilously incomplete. The institution of slavery lasted for over three hundred years, but freedom less than two hundred. The wounds inflicted during the former period will take considerably more time to heal. Meanwhile, Caribbean citizens have focused their hopes and ideals upon the vision of Toussaint L'Ouverture, who had set them on the path to citizenship and nation building exactly two hundred years ago.

The historicized imagination within which citizenship and nationhood were conceived and realized, has remained the dominant organizing force of Caribbean identity. Human rights progress is perceived in terms of flight from the scaffold of slavery and colonialism, and the universal wish is for full actualization of the popular refrain 'massa day done!' The journey to justice is idealized in a nationalist discourse within which the enslaved struggled to emancipate themselves, with some strategic support from metropolitan sympathizers. In the written history of these societies, the principal political colossus, the patriarch and matriarch of nationhood, are perceived as those whose political leadership of the marginalized and disenfranchised took on messianic proportions. *Up From Slavery*, the title of Booker T. Washington's classic autobiography, functions as the general theme and metaphor of widespread empowerment actions at all levels of popular mobilization.[1]

Ceremonial celebrations of emancipation were neither promoted nor officially sanctioned by the colonial state. Slave owners, as one party to the emancipation dialogue, were generally opposed to black freedom as a principle of social organization and economic development. For them, emancipation processes constituted a total undoing of the white supremacist order they had constructed over time with the full backing of imperial, political, economic and military might. In the British colonies slave owners claimed that the imperial government, in its commitment to emancipation, had betrayed them; they demanded compensation for the loss of property rights over their human chattels. Politically divided, but committed to colonial white rule, the imperial government capitulated and agreed to pay them £20,000,000 for their suffering. The blacks received nothing by way of compensation; their legal freedom was considered by all within the white communities as more than sufficient.

Whites who stayed in effective political control of the colonial administration, then, could not, and did not perceive emancipation as a movement worthy of official recognition. When blacks moved to develop their own programme to mark their freedom, it was received by the ruling class as an affront to its sensibilities and an expression of social insubordination and ideological revolt. For most of the nineteenth century this state of affairs was the norm. Some blacks made a joyful noise on August 1st, the date chosen by the British government to effect emancipation in 1838; most whites responded with a deafening silence. Mutual suspicion and distrust echoed through the corridors of public places, and the feeling that slavery could return was not far removed from the imagination of the blacks.

The effects of time were to reduce the pain rather than heal the wound. By the end of the century, fewer blacks came out to make merry on August 1st and it gradually declined as a day of celebration. The continuing hegemonic possession of economic resources and public governance

[1] Booker T. Washington, *Up From Slavery. An Autobiography* (New York: Penguin 1986; originally 1906).

by whites ensured that emancipation celebrations would assume small scale ritualized forms of resentment rather than radical micro-reconstruction. Only a few organizations on the radical fringe of the black political spectrum kept vigil; their members eagerly awaiting the resurgence of a popular movement dedicated to African redemption.

The centenary of the abolition legislation provided a compelling context for the emergence of refashioned concepts of emancipation as a long term sociopolitical process. Between 1934 and 1938 working class communities throughout the Caribbean were mobilized by radical political organizations – essentially trade unions and workingmen's clubs – but driven ideologically by the concept of black political enfranchisement. The Abolition Act of 1838 was represented as the harbinger of social enfranchisement; the attainment of universal adult suffrage a century later, took centre stage as the next phase in the process of 'emancipation in action'.

Labour rebellions spread from colony to colony during the mid-1930s. Their objectives were sufficiently clear to convince the imperial government that the minimally modified post-slavery colonial dispensation was no longer politically viable. Constitutional reforms, more liberal than radical, were presented by defenders of Empire as the answer to mass unrest. Emancipation celebrations on August 1st became increasingly popular as a community activity, and constituted a conceptual focus around which the demand for adult suffrage was made. In addition, the attainment of citizenship was rooted politically in this wider ideological rhetoric of emancipation, and the concept of 'massa day done' served as a common cliché in the language of popular radicalism.

Emancipation celebrations often took the form of political discussions about civil rights, Afrocentric cultural shows and festive exuberance. They were usually preceded in the morning by mass worship in the Christian church which continued to divide, and be divided by the popular democratic struggle. But the demand for social justice via citizenship brought into being both the end of Empire and the creation of national independence. These sociopolitical developments meant that emancipation would be realized as a body of new constitutional arrangements that enabled mass empowerment.

Historicizing emancipation, furthermore, took various shapes within the all-embracing project of nation building. The many nation states that sprung from the plantations throughout the length of the archipelago, all claimed ancestry in the struggle against slavery and the victory that emancipation represented. When, as was the case in all but one society, slavery was abolished by imperial legislation, anti-colonial discourse presented the event as a consequence of

Marc Latamie (Martinique, 1952)
*Side Effect*, mixed media installation, variable size. Photo: DR – Johannesburg Biennale 1997

'Using the real value of the South African cotton, I bargained 1.5 tonnes of the raw material, which came from a cotton factory in the country. The installation was based on the famous painting by Degas, *The Office of the Cotton Trader*, 1873, which he made on a visit to New Orleans.'

Marc Latamie (Martinique, 1952)
*Fleur-de-Lys*, White refined sugar, 200 x 150 cm, Isle of Gorée, Dakar Biennale 2000. Photo: Orlando J. Britto

'There are three types of cells, sort of waiting-rooms prior to the final journey across the Atlantic. A room for *men* – A room for *women* – A room for *young girls*. I wanted the white, refined sugar to mark the dark, earthy ground with the powerful emblem that was used on the Gorée flag, as well as on the Mauritian flag, during the French colonial rule.'

Marc Latamie (Martinique, 1952)
*Saint Mauricius*, Golden Statuette, 20 cm. Photo: Marc Latamie

'Started in 1992, this is a recurrent project generally used like a project currency. Obviously linked to the famous tragedy of the African Martyr who travelled through Europe, I used this small glittery object to represent the manufacture of trade*. Invariably the sculpture is adapted to fit the various spaces I am invited to present my work in. *The silver statue of St. Mauricius was cast in 1520 but was melted down to make silver coins twenty years later.' [Texts: Marc Latamie]

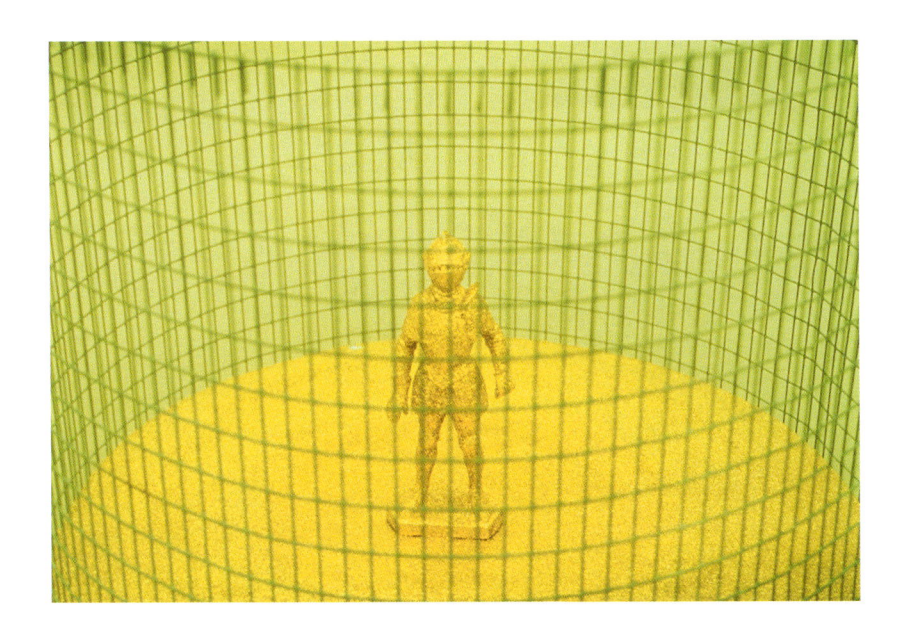

XXIV    Fine Arts

Godfried Donkor (Ghana, 1964)
*Pure Ali*, mixed media on paper, 38 x 50 cm, 2000

Godfried Donkor (Ghana, 1964)
*Black Madonna*, mixed media on paper, 38 x 50 cm, 2000

'Godfried Donkor's series *From Slave to Champ* (1996-) presented at the art Biennale Dak'Art 98 have caught the attention of a large crowd at the visual arts Panafrican Festival Slavery, a crime against humanity is revisited and dealt with by the artist, in a simple and clever composition, as a body of recollections whose strength has enabled the emergence of a new black consciousness, with the fierce determination and pride to conquer with intelligence, in the field of the "noble art", a new place in society. [...] By discovering afterwards Gorée Island in Senegal, mankind's world heritage – with it's numerous "old houses" full of so many stories of slave lives, but also fortuitously the richness and the strength of traditions that surround the traditional wrestling bouts 'lamb' in wolof. Godfried Donkor could not resist the temptation of taking the starting point of *From Slave to Champ* and extending it, in Africa, into a questioning of the rituals, the theatricality, and historical and magical/religious framework that turn Senegalese wrestling arenas into places of artistic expression, where the winning of social prestige is based on courage, cleverness, intelligence, strength and an insatiable lust for success.' [Extract from: Ousmane Sow Huchard, 'A testimony to the power of recollections and traditions' in: *Lutte traditionelle et mysticisme*. Dak'Art 2000, 2000]

Chris Cozier (Trinidad, 1959)
*G.N.P.* (Gross National Product), mixed media installation, 1999

'G.N.P. (Gross National Product) is really an interpretation of an island... black male and female genitals...sand...one box contains sugar and the other has white powder which alludes to cocaine...it is about raw materials for consumption and for export...the men with the briefcases are in a race running West, somebody has to win ...has to be ahead....the runaway is scattering away from the island to various locations...I liked the fact that the installation was on the old wooden floor of a sugar factory...' [Text: Chris Cozier]

Chris Cozier (Trinidad, 1959)
*Running man*

'These are the 3 rubber stamps. "Running man" and "Winner takes all" are appropriated from 19th century engravings. The other "And he was such a polite boy" was created by myself. The three create a narrative… owner man, migrant, and economic planner on the run…. They are the flags in "G.N.P."' [Text: Chris Cozier]

Chris Cozier (Trinidad, 1959)
*Winner takes all*

'Some of the drawings have been created with or from three rubber stamps. One, which I designed, with a "Running man" in a suit (heading for Switzerland) and the others, an "owner man" co-opted from historical engravings of landowners and another of the "run away slave" addressing the idea of migration … to me these images define the condition or historical origin of these islands.' [Text: Chris Cozier]

Fine arts    XXIX

Chris Cozier (Trinidad, 1959)
*And he was such a polite boy …*

Carrie Mae Weems (U.S.A., 1953)
Detail from *Here I Saw What Happened, and I Cried*, installation of monochrome C-prints
With sandblasted text on glass, 26.75 x 22.75 cm, 1995

'Weems begins her journey of traces in the Americas, in the Sea Islands off the coast of Carolina, where perhaps the strongest chords between African and the Africans in the New World may be found outside of the Caribbean. She goes in search of the Gula, descendants of the last batch of slaves out of Africa, who have in their secluded island retained strong references to the cultures of their origins. [...] In the installation, images of the slave experience are arranged and enclosed between identical images of an African woman who, head held high in anguished nobility, looks upon those evidences of historic injury and echoes Weems' title, "From Here I Saw What Happened, and I Cried." The anguished yet stoic woman in Weems' work is Africa, looking over the anguish and trauma of the Diaspora that was wrenched from her. In her poise she recalls the Biblical woman of Judea grieving for her children, and she will not be consoled.[...] [Extract from: Olu Oguibe, 'Slavery and the Diaspora Imagination' in this book.]

Marcos Lora Read (Dominican Republic, 1965)
*La Calimba* (series of five), iron and print on glass, life size, 1993
*La Marca* (series of five), fire brand on wood, 30 x 24 x 4 cm, 1993

'The work *Calimba* (Isometric games) refers to the significant year 1493 or the arrival of the first blacks to the American continent. In this case, the use of an historic date did not make the artist a mere chronicler; his works pose so much more, which stems from the way Lora Read conceives his rational aesthetics: "For me material and ideas are like liquids; they adopt the form of the receptacle that contains them". The original meaning of "Calimba" as an instrument with which slaves were branded, was extended until reaching a metaphorical dimension for the descriptions of racial traits and places of origin that classify us in identity papers and passports, wich explains the use of isometry as a conceptual game that begins with the very title of the work.[...] In his works, the objects became concepts, and autonomously reached a cultural and symbolic dimension. With them and the materials and the techniques involved, Marcos Lora Read questioned history as a progress in third world notions. His works are inspired by an anthropologic trauma of the Caribbean, to which he refers with metaphors and allegories. Quoting the language of the past, recovered and renewed according to today's perspectives, was fundamental in this work.'[Exracts from: Yolanda Wood, 'Thinking over History; the canoes and calimbas of Marcos Lora Read in Havana.', in: *Marcos Lora Read. Works 1992 – 1997*, Van Reekum Museum Apeldoorn, 1997]

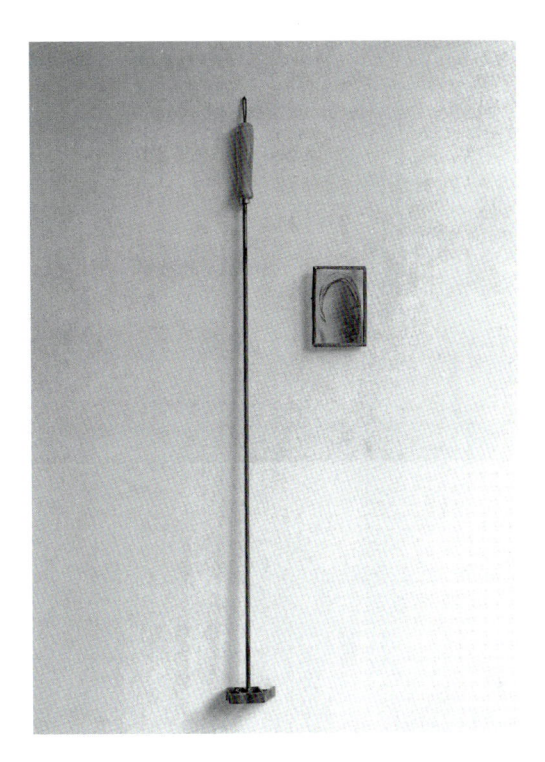

Keith Piper (Malta, 1960)
*Go West, Young Man.* Series of photomontages, 14 panels, each 55.8 x 35,5 cm, 1988 (Photo: courtesy of the artist and the Lux Centre)

'In *Go West, Young Man*, Piper aptly deals with slavery – and the will to enslave – as a lingering terror that manifests not merely in the denial of physical liberties but also in the surveillance and encroachment of social and mental space, also. He locates slavery both in the past and in the present. Like Bob Marley and Malcolm X, Piper reminds us of the reality and danger of mental slavery as part of the lasting damage which slavery and its legacies wreaked on both the African, and his adversaries. Though not directly, Piper's work nevertheless points us to the fact that the mind that succumbs to the fantasies of others is no more damaged or enslaved, than that which thrives on loathsome fantasy. We glean, by reasonable stretch of our own faculties, that slavery is a double-edged sword; it debilitates those whom it subjects to physical deprivation and abuse as much as those who perpetrate it. Time and history have left none wiser.' [Extract from: Olu Oguibe, 'Slavery and the Diaspora Imagination' in this book.]

popular rebellion and mass refusal. The new nations enshrined the heroes and heroines who had fought against slavery and its post-emancipation structures.

The political significance of over a dozen nation states claiming origin from within the ideology of anti-slavery, constituted a major expression of Atlantic modernity that projected emancipationism as one of its glorious philosophical movements. That enslaved blacks should wrestle with Eurocentric visions of Enlightenment and emerge as leaders and founders of democratic nation states, must surely constitute a most revolutionary development within this modernity.

Jamaica moved most rapidly along the contours of this discourse. Here for example, national independence was symbolically enlivened by the establishment of a pantheon of national heroes and heroines – all radical challengers of the colonial order. First, there is Nanny, leader of a Maroon clan that launched a protracted war against British troops in the mountains above the plantations; then there is Sam Sharpe, leader of the 1831 slave revolution; and following in this tradition, Paul Bogle, the peasant leader, and his mixed-race respectable supporter William Gordon, who inspired the struggle for black land ownership in the 1865 rebellion.

Recently, in 1998, Barbados, perhaps the most politically conservative of Caribbean countries, moved in the direction set out by Jamaica and officially recognized its national heroes and August 1st as a national holiday. The first three of these national icons, Bussa, Sarah Gill and Samuel Prescod, were all freedom fighters during the slavery period; Bussa led the 1816 slave rebellion, Gill used the Methodist pulpit to denounce slave owning, and Prescod built an alliance of free blacks and coloureds and liberal whites, to undermine slavery and to criticize post-slavery restrictions placed on the emancipated.

Other societies like Guyana, Grenada, Dominica and St. Vincent have also recognized their anti-slavery revolutionary leaders in the struggle for civil rights and their visionaries of national independence. In Guyana, a statue of Kofi, leader of the 1763 slave rebellion, occupies a central place; Bussa in Barbados is made to look out over the prime sugar plantation lands with broken chains in a posture of rebellious animation. In Jamaica, a national heroes' circle has long existed, and at this time there is public debate about the creation of a heroes' park where monuments can be displayed.

The message emanating from the celebration of these historical figures, particularly on August 1st, is that 'massa day is done', and that the process of redemption – from plantation slave and petty peasant to Parliamentary Prime Minister – is now complete. Despite the pervasiveness of this thinking, and the successes of the independence movements, some people in the Caribbean however, still remain trapped in colonial relationships. They are powerless with respect to resource ownership, and their economies cannot independently sustain adequate levels of material living. With regards to this, the point should be made, that those who govern are not those who rule. Ethnic minorities who arrived during the post-slavery period have inherited and accumulated a disproportionate share of the scarce resources, leaving behind the concept of black economic exclusion as a living reality. The historical forces of continuity and change suggest that the overlap of modernity in crisis with postmodern discourses are creating new conceptual frontiers for theoretical analysis in the region. While one group of citizens (whites) celebrate 'Discovery Day', and another (blacks) 'Emancipation Day', the most recently arrived groups (Asians) have now projected 'Arrival Day' onto the Caribbean/Atlantic canvas.

Olu Oguibe

## Slavery and the Diaspora Imagination

> Do you remember the days of slavery?
> And they beat us
> And they work us so hard
> And they use us
> Till they refuse us.
> Burning Spear, *Slavery Days*

In *The Atlantic Sound*, a travelogue of memory that takes him from England through the Caribbean back to Africa on a triangular reenactment of an earlier, historic embarkation, the novelist Caryl Phillips returns once more to a theme that has preoccupied his literary imagination and energies from his first book – published almost twenty years ago – to the present. This theme, which is anchored in the depths of the Atlantic Ocean, is not Phillips's alone, for it has equally preoccupied so many others since the aristocratic abolitionist Olaudah Equiano published his memoirs in England in 1799. It is the theme that will not go away, the theme that memory will not discount. Like others, Phillips clings to this theme, and the long memory around which it is entangled, as he journeys physically and spiritually through the geography of its perpetual burden. On one hand his mission is to comprehend an experience that is nevertheless incomprehensible. On the other it is to heed a call in the blood of all those who have come to inherit the brand of history, those who, having suffered so, must guard against history's propensity to repeat itself. Phillips returns to the theme of slavery and the journey of the African to the West because it is the duty of memory not to forget.

> 'History can recall, history can recall the days of slavery.'
> Burning Spear, *Slavery Days*

There is perhaps no other event in the history of the human species to rival in epochal monumentality, chronological spread, or sustained cruelty, than the African experience of slavery in the New World. And no theme or historical event has preoccupied the manifest imagination of the diaspora born of that cleavage of history, across nations and generations, with as much vigour and persistence, as the enduring reaches and ramifications of that experience. In literature, music and visual culture, in religious manners and traditions, in the conduct of social relations within and across race and blood, the memory of slavery remains indelibly fresh and present. Slavery, the Middle Passage from Africa to the New World, and the curse of diaspora, constitute the spine of the grand epic of the African sojourn in the Western world. The devastation of entire peoples and cultures, the psychic scar of a horrific journey away from the familiar and across the bottomless sea to centuries of brutal subjugation and disenfranchisement, explain the persistence of memory around slavery.

It is a persistence born of anxiety and a lingering sorrow: the knowledge that between the inheritors of this legacy a crater exists which time cannot fill; between, as it were, the descendants of the master, and those of the slave. But even more so, this anxiety is riveted on the perpetual palpability of slavery as a lived experience, as a terror that survives and mutates and re-inveigles the present. To the trauma and its incomprehensible past is added the horror of its omnipresence, which is underlined by the fact of its feasibility. Because such heinous action defies comprehension, those who inherit the scar of collective memory are placed in an ambivalent relationship with the rest, especially with those who have proven that beneath the veneer of sophistication and civilization that cloaks our species, lies a savage propensity to perpetrate the unnamable.

> 'I brothers feel it, including I sisters, too.'
> Burning Spear, *Slavery Days*

This persistence – this longitude – of memory is as evident in the contemporary art of the African diaspora today, as it has been for centuries. We find it in the work of artists such as British conceptual artist Keith Piper, who in the eighties, at the height of the most radical phase of his practice, devoted a significant body of work to the theme of slavery and its implications for the present. In *Go West, Young Man*, a series of photomontages produced in 1988, Piper, like Phillips, traces his own journey to the moment of embarkation on the voyage of the Middle Passage. (See page XXXII). In the text that appears on one of the panels of *Go West, Young Man*, Piper writes:

> 'I thought for a while / "Go West, Young Man". I first heard that joke / as they loaded us into / the hold of the ship / (checking our skin for lustre / & our limbs for muscle)'

From the 'Gate of No Return' on the African coast, Piper follows the slave ship to the Americas, and then to the plantations where, for the next several generations terror is visited on his kin. He writes on another panel of *Go West, Young Man*:

> 'I remember how they / pruned me with shackles/ &
> purged me with ritual castration…we had been
> reduced to / objects of fear and fantasy.'

In time physical visitation of terror is translated into the social and psychological as the descendant of slaves is driven under the shadow of derogation and stereotype. In the second part of *Go West*, Piper's protagonist emerges from the horrors of slavery and the plantations, to become slave to the master race's conflation of loathing and lust. He becomes, as Piper aptly describes it, 'fear & fantasy come home to roost'. In a scenario that recalls the writings of Frantz Fanon and James Baldwin, Piper writes in another panel of his work: 'I began to picture myself as they (hoped) to see me: The Body Beautiful Brutal!' 'It becomes worse', Piper's protagonist writes: 'It goes to my head.'

In *Go West, Young Man*, Piper aptly deals with slavery – and the will to enslave – as a lingering terror that manifests not merely in the denial of physical liberties but also in the surveillance and encroachment of social and mental space. He locates slavery both in the past and in the present. Like Bob Marley and Malcolm X, Piper reminds us of the reality and danger of mental slavery as part of the lasting damage that slavery and its legacies wreaked on both the African and his adversaries. Indirectly, Piper's work points us to the fact that the mind that succumbs to the fantasies of others is no more damaged or enslaved, than that which thrives on loathsome fantasy. We glean, by reasonable stretch of our own faculties, that slavery is a double-edged sword; it debilitates those whom it subjects to physical deprivation and abuse as much as those who perpetrate it. Time and history have left none wiser.

> *'Some of us survive, showing them that we're still alive.'*
> Burning Spear, *Slavery Days*

American artist Carrie Mae Weems takes Piper's tropic journey to the beginning a step further by making a physical one instead, just like Caryl Phillips in *The Atlantic Sound*. In the soul of the descendant of slaves lies a void created by time and brutal severance from the geography of origin. The loss of the slave is indeed enormous and unparalleled, and there is no stronger marker of its enormity than in the fact that he and his descendants were forbidden to register or discover the exact truth of their beginnings. This means that the slave and generations of descendants after him were left in the suspense of history, wedged between worlds to which they must only aspire, but never fully subscribe. Caught between a past that is largely lost, and a present that refuses to be owned, this becomes the greatest curse of the African diaspora: this unhinging from the past, this unknowing which results in a ceaseless, yet futile, effort to return, to seek for markers of origin, to know. The child of the slave seeks to assuage the collective trauma of her race by searching for nodes of identity and reunion, so that perhaps, through her, the souls of her ancestors may find peace.

Weems begins her journey of traces in the Americas, in the Sea Islands off the coast of Carolina, where perhaps the strongest chords between Africa and the Africans in the New World may be found outside of the Caribbean and Brasil. She goes in search of the Gula, descendants of the last batch of slaves out of Africa, who have in their secluded island retained strong references to the cultures of their origins. In a series from the early nineties entitled *The Sea Island Series*, Weems observes that the diasporic desire to discover Africa must begin in the diaspora itself, where traces and slivers of the past survive. She also makes a particularly notable point, namely that this survival must be sought not merely in the tangible or the seemingly authentic, but in mutations also, for instance in the emergence of the Blues as a dominant genre in American culture. It must be sought in peculiar manners and gestures and ways of relating; and in names of unfamiliar origin, in styles of conversation distinct from that of the rest of America, in peculiarities of taste and aesthetics. In one of the works from the *The Sea Island Series* entitled 'Went Looking for Africa' (1992), Weems has a ceramic plate on which she writes:

'Went looking for Africa
found it
lurking quietly
along the shore
of the Carolines
the inland

of Georgia
the delta
of Mississippi…
the malls
of Newark'

In order then to truly reconnect with her source, the descendant of slaves must begin her search in and around her present, within herself and the specifics of her immediate locale and moment. Except, of course, that the immediate can only constitute the first stop on a much longer and inevitable journey elsewhere. Weems embarks upon this other journey in her next body of work, the *Africa* series, which takes her inescapably to Africa, albeit only through the meticulous archives of the conquering race. In the process Weems underlines another notable fact of the diaspora experience, namely that the tropes of her survival in the Americas are lodged not only in cultural retentions among the descendants of slaves, but also in the master's annals of their violation. Memory finds its anchors in unlikely crevices and interstices of history.

Carrie Mae Weems's project in the *Africa* series is one of recuperative history, a reclamation of narratives of origin within which the African in America may reinsert herself to counter a past of erasures. Weems employs both words and images to reconstruct the history not only of the slave, but also of the species as a whole, affirming where science insinuates that in Africa lies the beginning of the human race. She embarks on familiar exaltations of long-gone civilizations, so that the distorted narratives of the slave machine are contradicted with evidence of African nobility and grandeur. Yet her most powerful work in the series echoes Keith Piper's revisiting of the past as it casts its critical gaze across time and geography.

In an installation of photographic prints under text-inscribed glass entitled *From Here I Saw What Happened and I Cried* (1995-1996), Weems rummages through the archives of the Peabody Museum at Harvard University to exhume the face of her ancestors. (See page XXX). Through a strategy not unlike Piper's in *Go West, Young Man*, she recalls those dehumanizing registers under which her ancestors were placed and upon which the ideology of slavery was built. On a set of four photographs from the installation she re-inscribes the divisive hierarchies of the slavery machine: 'house', 'field', 'kitchen', 'yard', categories that claimed to provide selective benevolence where indeed there was none. In the installation, images of the slave experience are arranged and enclosed between identical images of an African woman who, head held high in anguished nobility, looks upon those evidences of historic injury and echoes Weems's title, *From Here I Saw What Happened, and I Cried*. The anguished yet stoic woman in Weems's work is Africa, looking over the trauma of the diaspora that was wrenched from her. In her poise she recalls the biblical woman of Judea grieving for her children, and she will not be consoled.

We find in Weems's engagements with history and slavery, several details of the diasporic psyche, among them a ritual yearning to reengage with that from which it was once dislocated, to bridge the gulf, as it were, between the present and the past; to find an anchor for memory. We are able to discern the contours of the void that the descendant of slaves must try to fill, in order to move on. In addition, we find in evidence that ambivalence which must define the relationship between the inheritor of the slave experience, and others. It is no happenstance that the most significant contemporary artists of the African diaspora are constantly engaged with history, especially as they live encircled by a culture of forgetfulness. In Weems's work, as in that of numerous others, we find a determination to keep in focus the memory of this collective, yet very private pain, but also to emphasize that the experience itself is indeed a shared one that inhabits the soul of the West.

' Try and remember, please remember.'
Burning Spear, *Slavery Days*

If slavery is a leitmotif in the imagination of the diaspora that it created, it is because, as the Africans say, a wound may heal but a scar does not. Indeed, with regard to the deep wounds of slavery, even the prospect of healing is doubtful. The return to slavery and to images and tropes of its lingering trauma reiterates that what was done cannot be undone, and that the memory of it must be kept alive so that both perpetrator and victim may live in the shadow of its knowledge. Only in this way may we guard against its repetition. In his song, *Slavery Days*, Rastafari philosopher Burning Spear pleads with his listeners to *try and remember*, to *please remember*, no doubt aware that a fickle memory is a sure pass for the return of evil.

The preoccupation with the past and the present shaped by that past, which we find in the work of Weems, Piper and other artists and writers who have no direct experience of slavery yet bear the burden of its memory, echoes Spear's anxiety. It embodies and projects the anxiety of all those who are forever lodged in the shadow of a past of terror. It goes beyond the quest to understand or merely articulate the horrors and losses of the past, and instead seizes on the power – and duty – of memory to serve as a deterrent. Even more so, it counts on remembering to prepare the survivor for the inherent unpredictability of history.

Writing on slavery, the young Afro-Scottish poet Jackie Kaye warns in one of her poems, that what has happened once could happen again. Against this frightening knowledge, memory becomes a weapon, a reassuring guard against forgetfulness and a relapse into vulnerability. Survivors both direct and hereditary return, if only through a metaphorical doorway, to engage history as victims of terror. For them repetition becomes a trope for the triumph of will over collective and epochal trauma, the triumph of memory over the terrors of the past.

References

Kaye, Jackie, *Other Lovers* (Blood Axe 1993).

Phillips, Caryll, *The Atlantic Sound* (Faber and Faber 2000).

Rodney, Winston [aka Burning Spear] and P. Winston, *Slavery Days* (1975).

# Allison Blakely

## Remembering Slavery in the United States

Slavery was abandoned reluctantly in the United States; its abolition was an unplanned consequence of bitter civil war where the states attempting to secede from the union comprised most of the states in which slavery was still practiced. The initial abolition decree did not apply to those slave states not in rebellion. This circumstance surrounding the legislated national emancipation which soon followed, should be kept in mind when reflecting upon the subsequent attitude in the United States toward slavery and the slave trade. While among the slave population emancipation brought unbridled jubilation, there is little evidence that there was general remorse among the white public about the two centuries of trade to America or the brutal institution it spawned and which was perpetuated for another half century after the trade was ended. There was only a recognition that slavery had become a widely divisive issue in the nation and that it no longer was considered essential for economic prosperity. The moral issues, although raised from time to time, had always been of secondary importance and remained so.

This scenario is, of course, not peculiar to the United States. However, what is unique, is that it is precisely in North America that – especially in the latter part of the twentieth century – the most attention has been devoted to symbolic remorse, reflected in a host of organizations such as museums and libraries, and in monuments of various types. At first glance this may seem incongruous, since only an estimated five per cent of the African slaves brought to the Americas were actually taken to North America. The flurry of activity here can partly be explained by the fact that the United States is the wealthiest and most powerful nation and can therefore afford it. Another reason is that the North American tendency to emphasize colour over class resulted in a more pronounced continuation of the legacy of slavery than in those societies which, though having racially mixed populations – Brazil being the main example – deliberately blur the lines connecting the descendants of slaves to their ancestry. In such societies, though discrimination persists in customs, it has until very recently been considered inappropriate to speak about that past order of society.

Probably the single most important explanation for the degree of attention to the issue in the United States, is that both the slave trade and slavery always stood in such stark contradiction to the ideals on which the American experiment was based. The great Enlightenment ideals which inspired such crucial documents as the Declaration of Independence and the Constitution did not mean to include women or the majority of the general population under the concepts of human equality or the franchise. The fact is, however, that those concepts were harbouring an irresistible logic which sooner or later would bring about greater liberalization. Never before had there been such a radical experiment as the American one in breaking away from the traditional authoritarian social order, which usually included even state religions. Over time it became increasingly apparent that new fundamental principles would have to be adopted, or the state would have to work toward its ideals or lose its integrity. This became far more than a philosophical issue after the Russian Revolution struck an even more radical chord globally, one that resonated extremely well among the majority of the world's populations, which chafed under Western domination. It is within that context, and specifically that of the Cold War, that we can best explain the wave of recent public initiatives addressing the legacy of slavery. Thus, it is not an exaggeration to say that in a metaphoric sense Africa herself has called forth much of this atonement for her children: the United States could not risk losing the propaganda war with the Soviet Union, which could have resulted in the new free African nations ending up in the communist camp, along with the abundant natural resources and markets of that vast continent.

The commemoration of slave trade and slavery in the United States has covered all aspects of this broad range of subjects. The phases of the historical experience usually designated for observance can be placed under the general categories of the Middle Passage, referring to the Atlantic shipment in which untold millions perished; the institution of American slavery; liberation struggles such as the Amistad mutiny and the Underground Railroad; and the civil rights movement. The forms of commemoration have ranged from statues and monuments to museums and plantation re-enactments. More recently some of these have been further reinforced by websites on the internet which are very educational for those who never visit the actual historic sites. Spilling over into the world of commerce, there are also cultural heritage vacation tours.

In the academic realm, acknowledgment of the need to address the legacy of slavery witnessed the establishment of college departments and scholarly symposia on Black Studies; the publication of countless books and articles; and the acceptance of the concept of the African diaspora. The proliferation of Black Studies programmes and departments peaked in the 1970s on the wave of student protests in the 1960s and 1970s. The unprecedented numbers of black students in institutions of higher education was another part of the Cold War commitment for maximal mobilization of human resources in American society. After that time, the number of black studies programmes fell sharply, in part as a result of not having received complete institutional status, and in part due to shrinking educational budgets. In contrast to this trend in academe, there has been a conspicuous increase in the number of public museums devoted to this part of the American past. In the political scene this was paralleled by the election of hundreds of black mayors and other public officials. A major reason for this is that, due to a temporary preference of whites for suburban living, the past three decades have seen black majorities achieved for the first time in many major cities along with a high level of black consciousness among black leaders.

It is useful to describe here representative examples of the numerous and diverse efforts which are scattered across the United States. Beginning with the theme of the Middle Passage, perhaps the most spectacular project of all was the Middle Passage Monument Project, officially launched in July 1999. This featured a symbolic water burial of a monument, designed to memorialize the millions of people lost in transport across the Atlantic, and to promote a collective healing from the ravages of slavery. An organization called the Homeward Bound Foundation, founded by Wayne James, chose the sculptor for the monument, Eddie Dixon of Lubbock, Texas, from an international competition among three hundred and fifty artists. Dixon's design features a 25-foot arch depicting scenes from African history in bronze relief; a 100-foot-long granite walkway with African symbols, names of ancient empires and significant names and dates; and at the end of the walkway an 18-foot, bronze female figure, arms outstretched in a welcoming manner. As part of an elaborate ceremony in July of the same year, this was all lowered to the floor of the Atlantic at a location 427 kilometers off the New York city's harbour. Participants in the ceremony included prominent clergy, political leaders, spiritualists and entertainers. While this monument will probably never be actually seen again, the project also plans to place six replicas on land between the years 2000 and 2006 in the six regions of the world where transatlantic enslavement occurred, namely Africa, South America, the Caribbean, North America, Central America and Europe. The project has been endorsed by United Nations secretary-general Kofi Annan, as a project that may 'help broaden the understanding of African cultures and the heritage of people of African descent'.

Within the project a tour has been organized which is called 'The Middle Passage Pilgrimage', for those who wish to retrace part of the path of the slaves torn from Africa. The project included a journey to the West African countries of Senegal, Ghana and Benin, with the purpose of providing a series of films, lectures and other related activities. One impressive, unrelated, existing illustration of a memorial to the Middle Passage is in Detroit Michigan's new Charles H. Wright Museum of African American History. One of the Museum's permanent exhibits is a life-size mock-up of a slave ship during the crossing, complete with statues of men and women.

The attention given to the institution of slavery itself began with academic studies and publications early in United States history, with those studies becoming more critical after emancipation. Many museum websites include links to these references and to various collections of documents about what has been described as America's 'peculiar institution'. Colonial Williamsburg, Virginia, a restored eighteenth-century town owned by a foundation of the same name located some one hundred and forty miles from Washington D.C., is the nation's largest living history museum. Every year more than 100,000 students alone come on tours to see what the country was like when it started to become a nation. Colonial Williamsburg also offers what it calls 'electronic field trips': interactive internet visits, which include a session on slavery, indentured servitude and apprenticeship among the options. Among the other numerous excellent educational exhibits at Williamsburg are the slave quarter at Carter's Grove. In a compound of four rough wooden cabins, the visitor is confronted with a vivid picture of eighteenth-century chattel slavery, with costumed 'slaves' carrying out the normal duties of that time.[1]

A number of such working plantations exist at historical sites in other parts of the United States. In 1994 Colonial Williamsburg caused a minor sensation in the press when it announced that there would be re-enactment of an actual slave auction. Interestingly, while an African American woman headed the production for Colonial Williamsburg, the most vocal critics were African American leaders, some of whom feared the mock auction would trivialize the historical reality, while others felt the spectacle could be demeaning for today's African Americans. The modest mock auction nevertheless went ahead, including, for example, sale of a carpenter together with his tools, and sale of a man and his wife separately. The protest subsided after some who had earlier protested admitted that the 'auction' probably served a positive purpose.

[1] www.history.org

Some of the black cast employed for the roles affirmed that they found it beneficial to remind the public of the inhumane nature of this institution, the impact of which is still being felt.

Another recent initiative exploiting internet technology, one which specifically focuses on the Atlantic slave trade, is a virtual museum called the Museum of African Slavery. Designed especially as a resource for primary and secondary school teachers and their students, its main purpose is to keep the memory of the experiences of the enslaved Africans alive. The site's author, Pier M. Larson, is a professor of African history at Johns Hopkins University. The material and interpretations he offers are based on his own lectures and on the latest peer-reviewed literature.[2] As has been noted, the more conventional African-American museums include presentations on slavery, either in their permanent collections or in special exhibits. Some also feature electronic virtual tours. Examples of outstanding museums of this type are the African-American Museum in Philadelphia, the Dusable Museum of African-American History in Chicago, and the National Afro-American Museum and Cultural Center in Wilberforce, Ohio.[3] This latter museum, which opened in 1988, has the distinction of being the first national museum of its kind; it is funded by federal and state appropriations and by private gifts. A legislative measure in Congress to establish a national Afro-American museum in the nation's capital has languished for many years; thus the endeavours at the local levels remain the most important.

The one federal government initiative that has achieved considerable success is that on the Underground Railroad. This loose network of routes and informal aid stations which assisted fugitive slaves – perhaps as many as one hundred thousand in the fifty years preceding the Civil War – has captured the imagination of the public and appropriate government agencies. In 1990 Congress authorized the National Park Service to study the history of this phenomenon, and to find ways to preserve its memory and meaning. The study was conducted over a number of years, in cooperation with an advisory committee comprised of experts in historic preservation, Afro-American and United States history, and members of the general public with special

[2] www.jhunix.hcf.jhu.edu/~plarson/museum
[3] www.libertynet.org/iha
www.dusablemuseum.org
www.artcom.com/museums

interest in the subject. Their final recommendations included several alternatives, ranging from a major centre to various more isolated sites, monuments, or tours. Pursuant to these recommendations, the National Underground Railroad Freedom Center has been established, based primarily on funding from the private sector, but in a close partnership with the National Park Service. It is intended to be a national education and distributive museum centre. Scheduled to open in 2003, it is being built on the central river front in Cincinnati, Ohio, one of the main cities through which fugitive slaves left the south. This museum is conceived in the same spirit as the Holocaust Museum in Washington and the Museum of Tolerance in Los Angeles. Although treating a painful past, one which nevertheless at times inspired heroism and cooperation between people of different cultures, the purpose of the museum centers very much on the present and the increasing diversity of American society. In other words, the lessons from the past will be put to use for the needs of today's society.[4]

Are there any lessons to learn here for a Western European country such as the Netherlands? The historical experience of the Netherlands with slavery and the slave trade was of course quite different from that of North America. However, the interest of the Dutch parliament in making a significant national gesture concerning this dark chapter of history seems timely and appropriate. Since slavery was not allowed in the Netherlands, there is no tradition there of racial conflict and legal racial bias. However, the recent arrival of the descendants of slaves from former Dutch colonies is a reminder that the Dutch did have a role in this Atlantic trade and the institution of slavery in the Americas. At the same time, the even more recent arrival of additional tens of thousands of other black Africans is also a reminder that Dutch society will not be able to ignore the sentiments fostering black consciousness which are inherent in such populations.

The recent, admittedly scattered, protests against *Zwarte Piet* in the *Sinterklaas* tradition are one clear indication that different voices are present. The programme of the fiftieth Anniversary celebration of Leiden University's *Afrika Studiecentrum*, held in December 1998, featured a map showing that it is now possible to identify the Dutch cities with the greatest concentrations of the respective African communities. Some people present at the celebration already had ideas for establishing new cultural centres or museums highlighting their cultures. It will probably be to the advantage of the Dutch government to take a cooperative, leadership role in helping to

[4]
www.undergroundrailroad.com/gateway

bring these about. The experience in the United States with such institutions is that they have proven to be very valuable educational instruments, and foster cultural pride and high morale. It has also been proven that self-pride accompanied by sound education usually promotes better attitudes toward diverse cultures. For today's general public in the Netherlands slavery and the slave trade will seem much more remote and unfathomable than for the American public. Therefore, it is hard to imagine any type of single monument which will convey an understanding to the Dutch public. It would seem that some sort of educational centre or museum on slavery might best acquaint them with the issues and help them to understand why all peoples everywhere should vow that such a disgrace will never again occur in human society.

Seymour Drescher

# Commemorating Slavery and Abolition in the United States of America

Slavery has probably occupied a more central role in the historiography and popular memory of the 'first new nation' than in any of its counterparts in imperial Europe. Moreover, American historical memory focuses primarily upon slavery within the confines and coastal zones of the continental United States. Monuments, museums, commemorative plaques, urban areas and memorial parks are being created and modified at an unprecedented rate. From reconstructed Jamestown to new centres of scholarship, the history of slavery is being endlessly reconstructed.

American colonial governments were not among the principal political powers who sponsored the coerced migration of Africans to the Americas, and the transatlantic slave trade played a relatively minor role in the growth of North American slavery. Nevertheless, the institution of slavery was deeply embedded in the laws, and in the collective imagination of colonial Americans long before the creation of the Federal Republic. The growth of slavery was fundamental to the new nation's self-image and to foreigners' judgements of our society. Slavery's abolition, following the deadliest conflict in American history, was envisioned as a traumatic second birth or revolution. The flawed aftermath of Reconstruction continues to haunt us.

Until fairly recently, the memorialization of slavery's heritage was articulated primarily in terms of the history of its non-slave populations, the masters and the abolitionists. The principal sites of memory were reconstructed Colonial Williamsburg, renovated plantation mansions and Civil War battlefields. Only in the wake of the Civil Rights era, two generations ago, along with the infusion of African Americans into major political positions and higher educational institutions, did the black experience of slavery and freedom become a significant project in the memorialization of American history.

Initially, the institutionalization of the African American historical experience came primarily in the formation of departments of Black or African studies at colleges and universities and through stronger infusions of the history of slavery into public school curricula. During the past two decades other academic initiatives for the recovery and presentation of the African American experience have also emerged. The W.E.B. Du Bois Institute for Afro-American research was founded in 1975. It was the nation's first research centre principally dedicated to the scholarly study of Africans and African Americans. Affiliated with Harvard University, the Institute has funded hundreds of fellowships and created an academic network extending into Europe, Latin America and Africa. It has also sponsored the creation of a vast slave trade database. It has recovered records of more than 26,000 transatlantic slave voyages from Africa to all parts of the Americas. The most recent of these research institutes is the Gilder Lehrman Center for the Study of Slavery, Resistance, and Abolition at Yale University. Under the direction of prize-winning historian, David Brion Davis, the Center will hold international conferences on comparative slavery and abolition, fostering interdisciplinary scholarship on slavery and reform movements, as well as sponsoring seminars on the representation of slavery in popular culture.[1]

Significantly, the above mentioned two Centers are attached to two of the most prestigious private universities in America. They are, in a sense, monuments of scholarship to the history of Atlantic slavery and liberation taken as a whole. But the commemorative impulse has spread to institutions of popular orientation as well. American museums have traditionally devoted little attention to the development of slavery and to the experience of the enslaved. However, a new National Underground Railroad and Freedom Center will be opening in a few years in Cincinnati, Ohio. Involving both scholars and businessmen, its focus will be on the combined struggle of the abolitionists and the enslaved.

In the meantime, two American historians (David Brion Davis and James Horton) have also become advisors to a travelling exhibit on the abolitionist struggle, 'Free at Last'. It is circulating through fifty major libraries and other major centres in the United States. Older museums, not specifically dedicated to the experience of slavery, have also begun to increase their attention to this theme. New York's South Street Seaport Museum opened an exhibition on 'Transatlantic Slavery: Against Human Dignity'. Its format is modelled on that of the Liverpool museum of slavery in England. The exhibit will also go on tour: another example of mobile memorialization. As with many other emotive topics, this explosion of slavery memorializations has generated a good deal of cultural fall-out. A controversial slavery museum has opened in Detroit, reflecting a measure of Afrocentric ideology. Few if any scholarly experts were involved in its creation.

---

[1] I should like to thank Professors David Brion Davis and David Eltis for sharing their detailed knowledge about the Gilder Lehrman Center at Yale, and the Du Bois Institute at Harvard.

Through new sites of communication, such as email and the internet, groups have also attempted to reconfigure the meaning of older historical monuments. For example, a University of Colorado website, commenting on the Statue of Liberty, has carried statements that the original model of the Statue, gifted to America by France in 1886, was a Black woman. This model supposedly had been chosen by its designer in recognition of the unacknowledged 'fact that Black soldiers won the Civil War'. The website conclusion was that the Statue had been purloined by white racialist or immigrant groups. It was further claimed that the original model was housed in the Museum of the City of New York. In response to this assertion, the Museum, deluged with inquiries, had to create a dedicated mailbox to deny that any of its holdings could substantiate this account of the Statue of Liberty. It referred inquirers to the Statue of Liberty National Monument.

As a result, the United States National Park Service, custodian of the Ellis Island Statue, has launched a 'Black Liberty Project'. This project has two aims. The first is to trace the 'Black Statue' thesis back to its original appearance, or to the sources of the original claim. The Project's second aim is to prepare an account which incorporates all the layers of meanings and myths that have been added to the Statue's story over the century since its presentation to America. As with the academic centres described above, the Project's intention is twofold: to verify claims of fact, and to include the full story of African American challenges to racially exclusive narratives about the Statue's past history and current meaning. The Project will thereby test the extent to which competing claims about the Statue can be factually resolved without the subordination or inflation of African American claims. It will further analyze the degree to which a separation into 'black' or 'white' narratives is historically justified, and whether a truly synthetic narrative is intellectually feasible. The competitive commotion over the commemoration of the Statue of Liberty clearly shows one of the major ideological fault lines along which all attempts at memorializing slavery in the United States are likely to be divided.

Forms of rivalry may also emerge over other aspects of comparative commemoration. In the United States such a rivalry has been stimulated by the differential success of certain groups who had moved from positions of disabling social discrimination to rapid integration into American society. The successful launching of a number of Holocaust museums in major cities, above all, the Holocaust Museum in Washington, prompted some African Americans to aspire to parallel historical monuments, in order to evoke their own traumatic past. When commemorating the Middle Passage of the transatlantic slave trade for example, some African American scholars compared their effort to that of 'Jews who have vigilantly preserved memories of the Holocaust'. The commemoration of slavery has thus also taken the form of competitive victimization. At the extreme, this entails Holocaust denial or attempts to multiply the victims of transatlantic African enslavement to sixty or even six hundred million. One organization, the Nation of Islam, aimed to subvert the image of Jewish victimization altogether, by ascribing to Jews the primary responsibility for the transatlantic slave trade.[2]

This range of developments should alert planners of monuments and museums elsewhere to the potentially counterproductive aspects of institutional memorialization. Especially with a traumatic historical event or process, there is always a temptation for some to argue as though one could arrive at a hierarchy of collective suffering or radical evil so that only one such process reaches the apogee of uniqueness. This is a danger both for those who claim, as descendants, to 'speak for' the collectivity of victims and for those who, having no such claim, seek to defer to those claimants' vision in the interests of retrospective justice rather than greater historical truth.

In seeking to memorialize the history of slavery of other Western countries, such as indeed Dutch slavery, one might benefit greatly by carefully digesting the lessons of other such ventures. Slavery was less central in the development, and, even more significantly, in the collective consciousness of Dutch metropolitans. This may allow for a less polarized and disputable integration of slavery into Dutch memory. In fashioning a memory that integrates the voices and interests of many groups, one should attempt to be inclusive from the outset. In other words, procedural justice in the interest of creating an accurate historical record and not distributive justice, in the interest of creating a 'compensatory' narrative, may best serve the aims of memorialization.

Finally, planners of formal monuments for 'remembering' should themselves remember that, 'under the illusion that our memorial edifices will always be there to remind us, we take leave of them and return only at our convenience'. Monuments may 'become part of our past rather than a reminder of it'.[3] Monuments alone will not, in themselves, stimulate a constant rethinking of the past. That remains the task of historians.

2
See Seymour Drescher, 'The Atlantic Slave Trade and the Holocaust. A Comparative Analysis', in: A.S. Rosenbaum (ed.), *Is the Holocaust Unique?* (Boulder, CO: Westview Press 1996), pp. 65-85.
3
See James E. Young, *The Texture of Memory. Holocaust Memorials and Meaning* (New Haven: Yale University Press 1993), p. 5; and Tony Judt, 'A la Recherche du Temps Perdu', *New York Review of Books*, 3 December 1998, pp. 51-8.

Europe

# Frank Martinus Arion

## Un Beau Geste

Should the Netherlands make a healing gesture towards the peoples who suffered at their hands – victims of crimes against humanity and in particular of slavery? For many years this was a question which I considered only hesitantly. The answer became a certainty for me during the seventies, when I was working at the University of Amsterdam in the field of classical seventeenth-century literature. The way in which the students looked at me as they came in, at the beginning of lectures, was an indication to me of their confusion. It was obvious that in the sanctuary of what is known as the Golden Age they had not expected to be confronted with a very concrete result of that Golden Age: a brown-skinned individual of non-Dutch origin. I may add in connection with this – to the credit of the University of Amsterdam, and certainly of the revolutionary University of Amsterdam of that period – that during the years that I appeared in these lecture halls I was never openly rejected by any student. On the contrary, after each series of lectures I had gained a few good friends; some of them were even to become friends for life. It is true that on more than one occasion there were students who found it difficult to banish that veiled, pure image of the seventeenth century, cherished in their hearts until that moment, in order to replace it by a more realistic, browner image. Some of them denied responsibility for the dark side of the Golden Age, directly and with emotion. Often with the tormented rhetorical question: But I wasn't there, was I?

The answer is clear: No, of course not; nobody is responsible for the deeds of his ancestors, unless ... he accepts the inheritance of these ancestors. In other words, a Spaniard cannot be proud of the grand-scale discoveries of his ancestors without being ashamed of the equally grand-scale massacres of the indigenous peoples. Similarly, a Dutchman cannot boast of the achievements of the Golden Age without feeling a share of the responsibility for barbarous practices such as slavery, which make that Golden Age at the very least an alloy of gold and bronze. But in the final analysis it is not the heirs who are guilty, not the young people, but those who pass on this inheritance to them while concealing its real character and without paying the dues which they owe on this inheritance.

In the case of slavery – the greatest colonial crime – the dues arise from the fact that the slaves were never offered compensation for their suffering. In contrast to this, the state of the Netherlands actually paid compensation to the slave owners. To make matters worse, owing to the wrangling about the amount of compensation to be paid, the abolition of slavery even lasted a generation longer than was strictly necessary.

The older generation of Dutch people has so far not had the moral strength to come to terms with the past, which would enable them to leave a purer inheritance to their children. They also try to hide or camouflage past sins as much as they can. Or they resort to the tribal justification that what was done to other tribes – other tribes far away over the sea, moreover – in order to survive and raise children, should not be held against the forefathers. This justification, which assumes that it is permissible to do things to others which one would not like to undergo oneself, is unfortunately still prevalent in most parts of the world. It is part of the machete-wielding behaviour of the Hutus and Tutsis, of the Serbs and Croats, of the Americans with their bombers and the French with their nuclear tests. It is very far removed from humanistic behaviour, which specifically attempts to rise above tribalism and tries to treat people in distant parts as neighbours. Thus a healing gesture to the descendants of those who were unjustly treated in the past would mean being fully prepared to leave the tribal village in order to live in a wider world; accepting globalization, as it is called these days.

The Secret of the Concubines

Another example of cultural alienation resulting from concealment of the past is to be found in many of the Dutch nursery rhymes. Songs such as *Oze wieze woze, E pompei, Iene miene mutte* and numerous others are seen as anything but what they really are: Creole songs. In 1981 I wrote an article on this subject in the Dutch weekly, *De Groene Amsterdammer*. In appreciation of the publishers of the popular three-volume work *Kinderzang en Kinderspel* (Children's songs and games), I should like to mention that this article was immediately taken over in the seventeenth edition of this book, which appeared in 1982. I hope that a large group of Dutch people will now know that especially the most beautiful nursery rhymes do not derive from the Germanic pantheon, neither are they brilliant creations of nonsense-babbling babies. They are songs which Dutch fathers heard their Afro-Portuguese concubines singing for their brown offspring on the West Coast of Africa. When the fathers were back home again and the youngest (who had never seen papa) came to greet him after an absence of months, sometimes years, what could be nicer than to hear from papa's lips a new song as melodious as it was mysterious? Over the course of the years I have been able to gather an increasing amount of evidence indicating that my interpretation of these songs is correct. My fellow philologists still avoid the issue, in the hope that if everyone keeps quiet the golden colour of the past will be safeguarded against bronze.

The Secret of Literature

The best examples of contorted concealment and glossing-over of the bronze past are to be found in the field of literature. Countless reasons are put forward to explain the long silence of the famous Dutch writer, Nicolaas Beets, after the publication of his *Camera Obscura*. Not one single literary study, however, mentions the fact that Beets was a member of a society to promote the abolition of slavery, founded in 1853. Or the fact that between 1847 and 1857 he held at least three speeches against this barbarous institution. Due to this (deliberate?) lack of information, Beets is necessarily assigned to the genre of non-committal humour, where perhaps he in no way belongs. Take *De Familie Kegge*, for example, which was included in *Camera Obscura* in the third edition of 1851 and which had already been written in 1840. It becomes a more consistent story, a richer satire, if it is assumed that Beets had already taken a stand against slavery and slave owners before the publication of *Camera Obscura*. By seeking, in a contorted fashion, to keep slavery outside the nation's past and in particular outside 'pure' literature, *Camera Obscura* is deprived of much of its meaningfulness; and tedium within literature is augmented.

Political Suspicion

Lacking an attitude of unambiguous rejection of slavery, an attitude which can only be demonstrated by means of a *beau geste* or by *Wiedergutmachung*, the Netherlands remains an unreliable partner in a Kingdom now supposedly a partnership of three equals (the Netherlands, the Netherlands Antilles and Aruba). This suspicion is reinforced by the fact that the Netherlands was one of the last countries to abolish slavery, not doing so until 1863. This was fifteen years after the proclamation of the Dutch constitution. It should be noted that when the 150th anniversary of this event was celebrated, the Dutch minister of Interior Affairs invited the Netherlands Antilles to participate in the preparation of educational material for young people. It was not for one moment considered that this constitution of 1848 could have had absolutely no significance for the slave community of the Netherlands Antilles. The sheer effrontery of it! Moreover, the Netherlands made no haste as far as decolonization was concerned. On the contrary. The state plainly resisted it by waging war against Indonesia, after itself having felt the boot of oppression during the war. As far as Suriname and the Antilles were concerned, there was never much more than the bare bones of a Charter.

Thus the question is whether the Netherlands really wants to make new, democratic history in the new millennium, through deeds rather than words, or is it simply waiting for an opportunity to return to its old tricks? There is much suspicion, certainly regarding the Dutch attitude towards the Netherlands Antilles during the past decade. It looks as if the Netherlands has discovered the French decolonialization model, in which former colonies are completely incorporated into the mother country, with supposedly equal rights. There seems to be a haste to steer relationships within the Kingdom in the same direction. This great suspicion is nourished by the fact that the Netherlands was not straightforward in the way in which it put slavery and the colonial past behind it. There has never been a *beau geste* towards the descendants of victims of Dutch crimes against humanity, although these descendants sit daily at table with Dutch people. No one has ever said sorry. No consistent attempts have ever been made to compensate the people for the disadvantaged position in which they were placed. It is considered natural that the Germans and Japanese should make reparation (*Wiedergutmachung*) to their former victims, but the same idea is ridiculed when it concerns the Netherlands in relation to the Antilles and Suriname.

Monument

The Dutch government could take the first step in leading its own citizens towards openness to the past; it could take a first step towards concrete external *Wiedergutmachung*, not only to the Netherlands Antilles and Suriname but also to the whole West Indian world. This first step would be to place a monument, a monument against tyranny and oppression, against slavery in particular, a monument for human rights throughout the world, with the simple words: *never again*. It would be the counterpart, now lacking, of the memorial for the Second World War and the liberation of Nazi occupation on the Dam in Amsterdam. It would be a final farewell to destructive tribalism.

Translation Hazel Wachters

# Alex van Stipriaan

## The Long Road to a Monument

After years of more or less marginal attempts at making the history of slavery and its contemporary legacy heard in Dutch society, finally in 1998/99, the time was right and the issue took centre stage. On an international level, several activities in this sphere had proven to be quite successful, and in the Netherlands the lobby of black citizens and organizations had become sufficiently strong to forward the issue of founding a commemorative monument onto the national political agenda. This event was paralleled by the initiatives of several Dutch intellectuals. A few members of parliament actively supported this 'movement' and asked the Prime Minister formal questions about his ideas and plans on the commemoration of the slave trade and slavery in the Netherlands.

Some time later, in the Old Hall of the Dutch parliament, the presentation of the book *Het verleden onder ogen*, focusing on the necessity for a slavery monument, was attended by members of the cabinet and the Royal Family. This was another clear sign that the Dutch history of slavery was now officially taken seriously.[1] A further help, undoubtedly, was that the socialist-liberal government had made the multicultural society in all its aspects one of its priorities. Economic prosperity, moreover, made it possible to spend time and money on this project. One of the outcomes of these circumstances was the appointment of a minister specifically responsible for large cities and minority policies, who showed a willingness to listen to black organizations. By a favourite coincidence, one of the main advisors at his ministry was of Surinamese descent and in favour of a national monument. All in all, therefore, the time was right.

Upon opening the 'slavery dossier', one of the first problems the minister was confronted with was the diversity of black initiatives. Therefore, one of the organizations which had presented a petition to parliament about a commemorative monument, was asked to unite all initiatives. The minister reported to parliament that 'in principle the cabinet is willing to speak with a representative committee and the discussion may lead to the founding of a national monument to commemorate the abolition of slavery'.[2]

---

[1] Gert Oostindie (ed.), *Het verleden onder ogen. Herdenking van de slavernij* (1999). See also Adriaan van Dis, 'Coming to terms with the past', *Prince Claus Fund Journal 3* (December 1999), pp. 9-12.

[2] Letter to the chairman of the Lower House of the States General, May 26, 1999; [translation AVS].

The minister's request was only the final push in a process that had started long before that time: various organizations involved now quickly and easily formed a national Platform. Both Platform and ministerial staff vigorously went to work; within four months of negotiations – bilateral and unilateral – a first, detailed plan of action was presented to and accepted by the minister. Both parties agreed that the monument would have to consist of two elements. The 'static element', i.e. a memorial at a representative location, will intend 'to give to people a public place and symbol where the horrors of, and struggle against slavery can be commemorated'.[3] The dynamic element will consist of an institute aimed at coping with the history of slavery in a way orientated towards the future. According to the plan of action this institute will have a three-fold function: reflection, education and scientific research. All in all, these plans went a lot further than the mere creation of 'a national monument in commemoration of the abolition of slavery'.[4]

Hopes were high, and everything was geared towards unveiling the memorial at July 1, 2000, 137 years after the abolition of slavery in the Dutch Caribbean. However, since that date much time has passed. By now, the exact location of the memorial (in Amsterdam) has been established and nine selected artists, mainly from African or Afro-Caribbean backgrounds have submitted their proposals. It is, however, still uncertain whether the memorial will be unveiled before July 1, 2002. The opening of the institute will, no doubt, take place even later. Obviously, it will take more time (and money) to develop this element than to erect the memorial.

By now, we have probably passed the point of no return in relation to the two elements of the monument; the Platform has become the official negotiating partner of the government in all related matters and for the first time in history, the Dutch government has officially commemorated the abolition of slavery on July 1, together with the Platform. Still, one could wonder why, after more than a year of combined initiatives in a favourable political climate, no clear goals have been reached. The reasons for this are threefold and apply to both parties

---

[3]
*Van monument tot instituut: een schets op hoofdlijnen. Een nationaal monument in Nederland ter herdenking en verwerking van de slavernij.* Landelijk Platform 'Nationaal Monument Slavernijverleden' (August 1999) [translation AVS].

[4]
These changes, as well as discussions on what the Platform should be doing, are also reflected in the changing names of the Platform between its founding day, May 14, 1999, and the day it became a registered foundation: National Platform National Anti-Slavery Monument -> National Platform Commemoration Abolition of Slavery -> National Platform Commemoration Victims of Dutch Slavery Past -> National Platform National Monument Slavery Past and since December 8, 1999: Foundation National Monument Dutch Slavery Past, also known as National Platform Slavery Past, or just 'the Platform'.

concerned, i.e. the Dutch government and the Platform: fear of loosing touch with 'the people', division by 'professionalization' and 'officialization', and the clash of two opposing discourses. As will be shown hereafter, these three factors are closely interlinked.

As soon as the Platform was founded and talks with the government had started, the latter somewhat shrank away from what was set in motion. Time and time again the rhetorical question was asked, either implicitly or explicitly, whether the Platform was representative of the Afro-communities in the Netherlands. Of course it was not, the process of uniting all organizations[5] was – and still is – under way, not to mention the fact that there are some black people in the Netherlands who do not want to be reminded of slavery at all. However, the Platform made the effort to unite many ideologically and ethnically diverse organizations. This succeeded: within months, more than twelve organizations had joined the Platform, representing people of Surinamese, Antillean and Aruban, West-African and Amerindian descent, who were working on grass roots as well as professional levels. Although one organization decided not to join the Platform – it had been fighting for a slave monument longer than any of the others and boasts quite a large, mainly Afro-Surinamese following – during the negotiations its interests were also taken into account and it remained welcome to officially join the process. I was asked to become a member of the Platform to give my advise, despite the uneasiness some other members felt at first about the presence of a white professor of History. Therefore, it was unfair to blame the Platform for not being representative. What more could have been done?

    The real fear of the government was probably not the alleged unrepresentativeness of the Platform, but the feeling that they had 'created' a partner which could become much too radical to deal with, not to mention the consequence of having to promote such radical ideologies through a monument to Dutch society at large. As a result, the minister started distancing himself from the Platform by creating a rather autonomous Committee of Recommendation which was given the task to advise him and to promote the idea of founding a monument to slavery in society at large. This committee consists of intellectuals and artists – black and white. Its moderate views make it a buffer between the government and the Platform, which is probably exactly what the minister had in mind. However, since from the start the committee was never consid-

---

[5] At least three of these organizations are a union of organizations themselves.

Romuald Hazoumé (Benin, 1962)
Detail *La Bouche du Roi*, mixed media installation, 1999. Photo: Claude Postel

'To be aware of and to distinguish from the past has surely made it apparent that we should live together differently today. I see this as the message that lies within the installation entitled *La Bouche du Roi* by Romuald Hazoumé. This impressive work is not only a memorial to the victims: the slaves, but a monument that also pleads freedom as well as respect and dignity. It is a warning against all kinds of modern slavery – in its many variations. Forms of slavery that are more sophisticated than those of the past, that can provide fewer sleepless and less guilt ridden nights. The slaves in *La Bouche du Roi* each have a name and an identity and so have become individuals. However, they have their place in a certain context – in this case in a historical context. In its plea for individual dignity – but not without respect for others and with the willingness to take responsibility for society as a whole – *La Bouche du Roi* offers hope in the new millennium. As historical as the theme seems, *La Bouche du Roi* is about the present and perhaps even more, about the future.' [Text: Frits Bless, 1999]

António Ole (Angola, 1951)
Elements from: *Hidden pages, stolen bodies*, mixed media installation, 1996-2001

'At a certain level, it looks as if the war is over, which transmits a certain hope in the air… I'm finishing my work on slave trade in Benguele and a final visual/historical look at Angola in the last century. The project has been conceived in a multidisciplinary way. I'm using drawings, photos, some paintings, installation, sculptures, objects and some video projections.' [Text: António Ole]

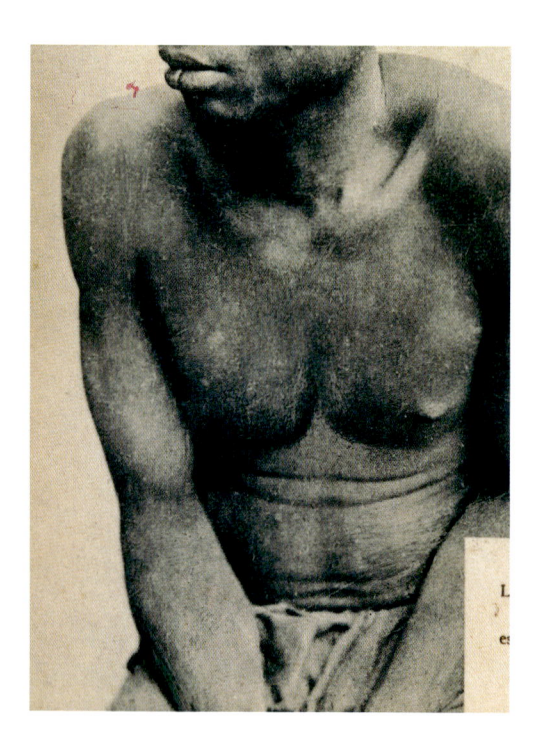

Maria Magdalena Campos-Pons (Cuba, 1959)
*Seven Powers that Came by the Sea*, mixed media installation, 1993

'Maria Magdalena Campos-Pons' body of work made over the past decade, since her immigration to the United States in 1990, makes real to her audience the history of black African migration to Cuba and the United States, and the contemporary multi-cultural and trans-cultural experience. Dislocation and diaspora influences on the artist and her family are the sources of her artistic reflection. Her work values women and celebrates their strength, awakening us to women's roles and points of view in society and their expressions in contemporary art. [...] In 1993, the artist performed the installation *The Seven Powers that Came by the Sea*, at the Vancouver Art Gallery, in Canada. Wearing a dress worn by the slave women of the 18th century, numbers were printed over her limbs in contemplation of the anonymity of the many nameless people that did not survive.' [Extract from: Sally Berger, 'Maria Magdalena Campos-Pons, 1990 – 2001' in *Authentic/Ex-Centric. Africa In and Out of Africa*, 2001]

Miguel Petchkovsky (Angola, 1956)
*The Cup of Tea*, oil on painted textile, 160 x 145 cm, 1998

*The Kingdom of N'Gola*
'In my country, Angola, which was party to 30% of the slave trade in Africa, strong references to slavery can be found everywhere and its memory is vividly passed down the generations through oral narratives. In my work I investigate how images can stimulate the creation of individuals' recollections of people in the past. Memory is an essential attribute of the human psyche and is therefore more personal than historical or material knowledge. History alone cannot enrich memory, because it is systematic and sequential. In my works I deal with images of the redefinition of the human body in a pre-dark age of slavery, the plundering of African spirituality (masks and ritual sculptures) and the fundamental influence of Christianity on the slave trade.'
[Text: Miguel Petchkovsky]

Miguel Petchkovsky (Angola, 1956)
*In Hoc Signo Vinces*, mixed media on wooden structure, 150 x 150 cm, 2000

Eustáqio Neves (Brazil, 1955)
Part of 'Objectization of the woman body' project, mixed media, Cibaprint copy, 80 x 100 cm, 1998
*Arturos*, toned silver gelatin print, 50 x 60 cm, 1994. The Arturos are a closed community named after Artur Camilo, descendant of slaves, who died in 1956, aged 76.

'During my residency at Gasworks Studios, London, I continued to develop the Slave Ship project taking Brixton as the focal point for my research on Black/African diaspora communities in London. The starting point of the Slave Ship project was a lithograph and the poem, Navio Negreiro (Slave Ship) by the poet Antonio de Castro Alves. Slave Ship aims to establish a relationship between the past slave market and the current global economy.' [Text: Eustáqio Neves]

Sue Williamson (South Africa, 1941)
*Messages from the Moat*, water, engraved bottles, net, pump, soundtrack, installation view, 1997. Photo: Archief, Den Haag, 2000

'From 1658-1700, the time of the rule of the Dutch East India Company (VOC), first colonizers of the Cape of Good Hope in South Africa, more than 1400 transactions involving the buying and selling of slaves were recorded. These records, supposedly the most comprehensive such records in the world, can still be seen in the Deeds Office, Cape Town. In *Messages from the Moat*, each of these transactions is represented by one bottle. (The 'moat' was the barrier of water which surrounded the Castle built by the VOC, and later dredgings found fine objects which might well have been thrown into the water by slaves kept inside the Castle). In the piece, engraved on the side of each bottle is the name of the slave, his or her birthplace (the slaves were taken from all up and down the coasts of Africa, India and the East Indies,) the buyer, the seller, the price paid in Rijksdollars, and the date. Treated as easily expendable commodities, in *Messages from the Moat* the slaves/bottles are shown being lifted from a sea of other bottles by an enormous net. The piece was conceived not only to recover a hidden history, but to consider the human price paid for amassing the wealth of 17th-century Holland. A small publication listing the names of the slaves and the details of the transactions accompanies this piece. Shown first at the Johannesburg Biennale in 1997 with its theme of "Trade Routes and Geography", *Messages from the Moat* has since travelled to Sweden and Holland and is now back in South Africa.' [Text: Sue Williamson]

Geraldo Steven Pinedo (Curaçao, 1958)
*Negroes for Sale*, silkscreen on linen, 145 x 100 cm, 1997/99

'For several years, Geraldo Steven Pinedo travelled around Venezuela, Ecuador, Colombia and the islands of the Caribbean, carrying out research in libraries and at the locations where the slave trade took place. During these trips, the artist had the painful experience of discovering that people in Latin American countries were no longer aware of their own roots, and did not regard themselves as descendants of slaves. In the course of his explorations, Pinedo inspected and collected countless documents. He acquired many examples of the instruments and equipment that was used to remove people from their ancestral homelands and to take them to a life of perpetual captivity. With this installation he has created a memorial to those who lived their lives in slavery and lost their lives in a condition of servitude. […] Pinedo relates the figures in his paintings to textual information. Careful lists of instruments of torture, shackles and iron collars are set alongside a metal mask for concealing a human face. Red, the colour of blood, symbolic of love and life, but also a signal for danger, the colour of radical change, of revolution.' [Extract from: Geraldo Steven Pinedo, 'The Past, Slavery, The Present, Culture', Gothaer Kunstforum Köln, 1999]

ered by anyone within or outside the Platform as 'we', but always as 'they', and vice versa, which complicated things immensely.

Apart from this, a steering committee was constructed in which representatives of several ministries, the Committee of Recommendation and the Platform participated. This steering committee is intended to be a forum where negotiations take place and decisions can be prepared under the supervision of the the minister's representative. As a result of this, the Platform was not only put at some distance, but also its delegates became more bound to the government's objectives, as content and fundamental discussion were more and more overruled by procedures, time schedules and budgets.

Meanwhile, the only ideology all organizations in the Platform had in common was the aspiration to give the history of slavery and its contemporary legacy a 'rightful' place in Dutch history and society by the foundation of a monument of two elements. All other questions, including the ethnic composition of the Platform, the contents of the monument, or the exact meaning of the legacy of slavery today, was, and for a great part still is, under discussion. This is exactly the reason why the Platform is representative, because it shows it is a platform for everything relating to this issue in the Afro-Dutch communities. These discussions are part of the process of coping with a history of slavery and racism. However, in delicate matters such as these, discussions and processes are far too complicated for a government to deal with. They need concrete opinions, which can lead to actual political results.

Under these circumstances, a situation has been created which is not at all encouraging any concrete results, precisely because there is not (enough) room for dialogue and debate. Not only has content been overruled by procedures, the debate also seems to have lost its dynamics, as a result of the diversity having been reduced to an institutionalised, two-party system. On the one hand you find the moderates, the Committee of Recommendation backed by the government, on the other hand the Platform, which has been – or has allowed itself to be – pushed into the corner of 'radicalism'. Hardly any substantial debate between the two takes place, and probably not even within the two. Both 'parties' take position and pretend to know how the other thinks.

This situation has been complicated by the fact that founding a commemorative monument, not to speak of founding an institute, or changing history school books, calls for long and complex judicial and official procedures, which are hard to explain to 'the public'. Moreover, part of the (mainly white) public is not interested in the issue at all, whilst another part – white and black – is interested, but wants it to be settled quickly, in view of the many other projects in multicultural society; yet another part of the (mainly black) public is mistrustful, fearing that white dominance is taking over by trying to 'whiten' black initiatives along the procedural way.

As a consequence of these developments, much time is devoted to formal discussions and procedural questions in settings which are far removed from 'the public', and too little time and energy is spent on communicating with that 'public'. The result is that the (opinion-)leaders in the process sometimes feel obliged to express firm statements, otherwise images of radicalism or conservatism are ascribed to them by others, in order to keep in touch with 'the people'. Consequently, schisms within the movement at large, and misunderstandings between the 'generals' and the 'troops' are an immanent danger and threaten the common goals and continuation of the process.

Despite all this, the realization of the static element of the monument, i.e. a memorial statue, has come into sight. But even in respect to this, a lot of issues still need to be solved. For example, whose monument is it going to be and what should it be an expression of? Such questions, when related to the dynamic element of the monument, i.e. the institute, create double the amount of discord. Will the institute, and the processes and debates it is going to initiate and stimulate, be primarily aimed at empowering the Afro-communities in the Netherlands, or will it be aimed at society at large? What kind of history will it be 'promoting'?
These and other related questions have to be answered or at least debated upon in an early phase, because they have already turned up today and they are fundamental to the dynamic monument. Terminology seems to reflect a clash of discourses in this respect. For example, in one discourse a deliberate choice is made to use phrases such as 'trauma' and 'detraumatization', 'black holocaust', 'reparation of history' and 'Afrocentrism' in order to be able to fight for the future. In another discourse the use of such phrases is absolutely 'not done', they are avoided at all costs and even talk of 'victims' or 'guilt' are considered to block the way to a more harmonious or open minded future.

It will be of crucial importance to understand why people are part of one discourse or the other, and why they experience and represent history, the present, and the road to the future the way they do. Without efforts towards an understanding and a respect for others, combined with a critical look at oneself, it will be difficult to erect a real monument.

Ruben Gowricharn

## The Creole Janus Face

As a child I lived in Poelepantje, a neighbourhood in Paramaribo separated from the southern districts by a canal. According to tradition, the name *Poelepantje* is a corruption of the command *Poer ie panji*, which means, 'Remove your loincloth'. Slaves who accompanied their masters to the city, or who were returning to the plantation, or anyone who wanted to cross the canal for whatever reason, had to swim across. This crossing place was infamous for the many deaths by drowning. There were also two important Paramaribo monuments in this neighbourhood: the majestic water tower, which still supplies the city's drinking water, and the second largest market in Paramaribo, if not the whole of Suriname, the *Kleine Markt* or Small Market.

The day the abolition of slavery is celebrated in Suriname, 1 July, is not simply a day-off, it's a national holiday. This is especially noticeable in the *Kleine Markt:* bands playing Creole music and Creole women dancing in traditional *kotomisie* dress dominate the scene. Typical too are the porters and odd-job men, and the numerous Surinamese soft drinks and snacks, which are handed out to everyone for next to nothing, including to the Hindustani, Chinese and Javanese people, who also watch the spectacle, though usually from a respectful distance. However familiar it all may be, celebrating the abolition of slavery continues to seem a little strange.

We all knew the terrible stories about slavery from school, not from our families or any other more direct source. Those of Asian descent arrived after slavery had been abolished in Suriname, so even a desire to identify with that particular past remained flawed. Moreover, in the time that followed there was little contact between the different ethnic groups. Up until the Second World War, they were economically and geographically almost entirely separate: the Hindustanis and Javanese were involved in agriculture, the Creoles in mining and forestry, or they lived and worked in the city. The postwar urbanization of the Asian groups led to a defensive adjustment. Although they became creolized through urban culture, and social contact was marked by playful stereotypes – which did not necessarily lead to social exclusion as it did in the Netherlands – they strikingly elected to maintain a cultural distance. This can partly be explained by the latent racial tensions, which could suddenly manifest in the streets or elsewhere, and partly by the scant understanding the Creoles showed of their own identity or culture, something the chauvinist 'Asians' found hard to comprehend.
For a long time the Creoles regarded their own folk culture with contempt, particularly the

better-off among them. In as far as a local form of *négritude* existed, it was primarily inspired by movements elsewhere: American Black Power, the South African anti-apartheid movement and the Afro-Caribbean varieties of Castroism. This elitist Surinamese nationalism went little further than lamentation and an inflated self-image. However, it did contribute considerably to the popularization of the existing folk culture, both of the city dwellers and those living in the interior. Nonetheless, Western supremacy remained unscathed.

This lack of a distinct cultural backbone was blamed on the devastating consequences of slavery. However, this accusation is not convincing simply because the Surinamese Creole wore a Janus face. On the one hand, there was the desirable white civilization with its education, healthcare, technology and capital. Everything white, or white-tinted – and this applies literally even to skin colour, which became a signifier of social position – was placed high in the hierarchy of colonial society. This colour hierarchy was not only the result of brutal violence, as the ideology of the victim would have it; loyalty and romance, hate and betrayal, goodness and moderation also occurred between slaves and masters, and between slaves themselves. Even though Surinamese mulatto culture has been inadequately recorded, there can be no doubt that lighter coloured descendants of the black Africans are proud of their upgraded skin colour and the status that this brings. By accepting this hierarchy, and by deriving pride and self-esteem from it, the descendants of the slaves lose their innocence.

On the other hand, the white man was put in place as the colonizer, slave master, exploiter and oppressor. These popular imputations are not always valid in Suriname because much that is of value emerged from Dutch colonialism: the level of education, health care, agriculture and, in particular, land reclamation, the development of the infrastructure and economic investment. None of this would have been possible without the contribution of the colonizer. Karl Marx was right when he said that capitalism increases the powers of production worldwide, but in Suriname this was not enough to generate any kind of surplus. On balance, the colonizer invested more in the colony than it ever received. Even the bloodbaths that took place in the struggle against colonial rule, insofar as such events occurred in Suriname, pale into insignificance when compared with the mass murders that have taken place and still take place in numerous Third World countries.

The first inhabitants of Suriname were the Amerindians, the second were the whites. This gives the whites, as Surinamese co-inhabitants, just as much historical right to voice their opinions. Moreover, the economic profit and the cultural and social mix are too great, too visible and too complex to be able to dismiss colonialism as a purely destructive force. V.S. Naipaul was mistaken when he said slavery in the West Indies has produced neither civilization nor ruins. Black slaves and white colonizers have had many faces, ranging from the enemy to the loved one. A nationalism fuelled by an analytical model consisting of white perpetrators and black victims is therefore too simplistic to sustain.

At present, the biological assimilation continues to an even greater extent in the Netherlands, where relationships between white Dutch and primarily Surinamese Creoles occur in great numbers. At the same time, the machinations of the military regime in Suriname discredited Surinamese nationalism, causing the social and psychological distance that nationalism had created in relation to the whites to instantly melt away. Whites and blacks are more and more content with each other. Most of them are unaware that they sleep with the colonial problem.

Even if these mixed-race couples are visible in contemporary urban streets, this development is primarily a *physical* mixture of black and white, and to a far lesser extent a *cultural* one. Missionary work, Western education and the continuing effects of colonial complexes have brought the 'civilized black' closer to the white. This 'cultural closeness' is so great that one can hardly speak of *mixing*. Even when creolization in language, music and dance is added to the mixture, the historical inheritance of a shared legacy remains meagre. This heritage might also have consisted of a research group 'sociology of the slave society' at Dutch universities, or the creation of a museum or statue in memory of this past. However, in history lessons the colonial past is brushed over; references to colonialism or slavery are felt to be politically provocative, and even literature has failed in this area. The inheritance of the Jews and the Indonesian Dutch shows a marked contrast. These groups can boast a 'subculture' which has a place in Dutch society.

A public debate on slavery is needed, not in order to derive the right to be an historical victim, but rather to be able to honour the ancestors, to acknowledge the suffering that was inflicted, or for the sake of atonement. This will not be a simple exchange of opinions. The roles of slaves and whites vary and the political claim that requires the other groups within the population to identify with this shady past is ambiguous. Moreover, the meaning of slavery goes beyond being the victim. Just as the persecution of the Jews placed questions of race, genocide and 'visible difference' on the political agenda, so slavery refers to current issues. Think, for example, of the superordinate and subordinate positions of people and world views, and the legitimization of the exploitation of coloured people. Or think of the Western civilizing drive which is still active in development practices. Not to mention the number of current subjects that affect multicultural society, such as the continued existence of racism, discrimination and prejudice; and the need to civilize the other to correspond with one's own image, or the lack of respect for those who look 'different'.

Not only are 'multicultural' subjects thematized, the reactions to them are categorized as well. The Dutch habit is well-known: to deny, ignore, play the holy innocent. These are and were the customary reactions, even in the time of slavery (which, by the way, was never entirely uncontroversial in the Netherlands). Current attitudes provoke tense reactions from other Dutch people: racial jokes, for instance, are taboo, and the behaviour of non-whites is often glossed over in line with the Dutch habit of cultivating victims. Surinamese reactions also need to be adjusted: no rights can be acquired by being a victim, nor is it appropriate to harbour an attitude of moral superiority. The disregard of Creoles for their own skin colour and the desire for assimilation into Dutch culture also belong on this list. Frequently heard statements like 'don't be so black', 'you need to raise your colour' or 'she's a beautiful black woman' always generate unease. As if 'black behaviour' is something cultural-pathological, the black colour inferior, or a black woman unlikely to be really beautiful.

From a biological and cultural point of view, it seems that the descendants of slaves are working hard to dissolve into the white world in much the same way as the Dutch Indonesians have assimilated. Like cultural or racial purification, cultural or racial mixing is an extreme development, particularly if it is carried out consciously and willingly. With this assimilation Creoles lose the right to call the whites to account. Their predilection for the 'Paradise of Orange'[1] cannot be reconciled with cherishing an identity as historical victims. On the stage of history, Creoles stand before the choice of either regarding whites as the enemy, or loving them. The Creole is naked once more; *Poer ie panji* still applies.

Translation Annabel Howland

---

[1] The expression is borrowed from a novel by the Surinamese author Bea Vianen, *Het Paradijs van Oranje* (Amsterdam: Querido 1973). The Dutch Royal Family bears the family name 'of Orange'.

# Harry Goulbourne

## African Slaves and the Atlantic World

If there is a collective national British consciousness about slavery it is that Britain has a proud record to boast. This record is Britain's commendable role in leading the crusade to end the trade in 1807, the noble and humanitarian efforts of men such as Clarkson and Wilberforce, the eventual abolition of slavery itself in 1834-38, and the navy's role in policing the high seas against those less than worthy nations that continued to trade in slaves. Additionally, Britain's role may be contrasted with Napoleonic France's attempt to reintroduce slavery in the West Indies, particularly in Haiti. In that country, Toussant L'Ouverture had established a state that slave colonies in the region, as well as the southern states of the new American Union, saw as a potential bridgehead for the freedom of Africans on that side of the Atlantic. As the debate over the relative merits of states' rights versus federal power, and free labour versus 'the peculiar' institution of slavery spread with the expansion of the American Union from the 1830s to the 1850s, and as slavery continued in large societies such as Brazil and serfdom continued in Russia, the British looked morally good. This 'goodness' has continued to inform the national psyche, and comparatively little has been or is being done to address or redress the monumental injustice of African slavery across the Atlantic world.

There are, however, some important parts of the story missing in this account of the nation's role. For much of the three or so centuries of slavery, the world experienced the first British empire in North America and the Caribbean, and Britain steadily established control of the main sea trading routes. Slavery was a major plank of John Bull's colossal presence across the Atlantic and in the Americas. More significantly, the Humanitarian Movement, as Eric Williams argued in his seminal work, *Capitalism and Slavery*, was less important than the emergence of the *laissez-faire* philosophy of the age epitomized by Adam Smith.[1] A new generation of hard-nosed entrepreneurs with keen interests in the riches of India and China had also appeared, for whom slavery and the mercantilist system were anachronistic obstacles blocking access to large markets. Initially a contributor to the early industrial revolution, the system of slavery had become a massive hindrance to the further development of industrial capitalism, and a combination of enlightened interest, evangelical humanitarianism, as well as slave rebellions and resistance led to the demise

---

[1] Eric E. Williams, *Capitalism and Slavery* (London: Deutsch 1981; originally 1944).

of the disgraceful system. For the most part, there have been almost two centuries of relative silence in Britain about the place of slavery in the nation's history and national consciousness. In very recent years, however, efforts have been made to re-awaken this aspect of the past as part of the national consciousness. For example, the major cities of Liverpool and Bristol, whose growth and prosperity have been intricately bound up with the slave trade, have sought to organize galleries and exhibitions around slavery. Such efforts must be welcomed and applauded. Indeed, there must be admiration for the courage and initiative of those, such as in Bristol, who stood up against people who would prefer to keep the whole matter under cover and continue the long historical silence about the disreputable past that several British cities and families share. These efforts are, however, inadequate as a recognition of that shameful past – a past that continues to cast a large shadow over our present condition.

This present condition is common to both native Britons and their descendants spread across the Western rim of the Atlantic world, and the descendants of Africans who share these parts of the world. Descendants of African slaves in the Caribbean, North America and Europe share this past with the descendants of those who benefited financially from the trade and the system in the Caribbean. A past which will continue to evoke a sense of guilt, shame and ambiguity.

In Britain, there have been those who enjoyed, and their descendants who continue to enjoy the fruits of slavery. Since the histories of individual families have not been carefully and rigorously related to that seemingly distant past, the nation as a whole remains ignorant of who they are. The general impression is that such families, and indeed sometimes whole communities, are too far removed from the present for the matter to be of any contemporary relevance. But this is not the case. When slavery ended, the British government made funds available to the former slave owners for the loss of their commodities (that is to say, their slaves, thus persons, human beings), whilst the former slaves were abandoned and left to fend for themselves in a less than friendly socioeconomic and political environment. These communities and families have never experienced the exorcism of the guilt that champions of apartheid in South Africa have been given the opportunity to exorcize. The few very little things that relatively fewer individuals (Baptists, Quakers, old-fashioned socialists, etc.) have undertaken, have therefore been portrayed as great acts of humanitarianism, thereby reinforcing the national feeling of well-being about slavery and the marginality of that part of the country's great history.

In many Caribbean countries, such as Jamaica where the slaves consistently challenged the system of slavery through rebellions as well as more subtle methods of subversion, the abolition of slavery has since long been annually celebrated. Throughout the region, the development of viable democratic social systems has been largely ignored by the wider world community, particularly by the former imperial powers. But even in these societies, the legacy of slavery has still to be squarely faced at the aggregate levels of society and state. To be sure, poets, novelists, academics, painters and so forth have all addressed the slavery past. But what this past means for the present patterns of ownership, social integration and control of social, economic and political power has not been squarely faced in terms of policy and public discussion.

In the last few years the Abuja Declaration of the Organisation of African Unity, calling for Africans to be compensated for the slave trade across the Atlantic, has been a rallying point for many who are concerned about this long and unjust neglect of the victims of slavery. I cannot say that I understand, or have much sympathy with the claim being made. But I do understand that the claim involves recognition on the part of Europeans of the historic suffering that specific economic enterprises, with the support of their respective governments, inflicted for gain on a people, for which their descendants should be compensated. Proponents of reparations draw on the experiences of Jews under the Nazis in Hitler's Germany, including the compensation that Germany has been making to the state of Israel, and the compensation made to specific families by Swiss banks. Similarly, the compensation of American Japanese families who were interned during the Second World War has been pointed to as a model to be emulated. The issue of compensation, however, will long exercize the minds of thoughtful individuals on both sides of the divide. After all, reparations raise questions about morals and ethics as well as about political expediency.

In my view, these demands, like the well-intended and salutary exhibitions in British cities, do not satisfactorily address the central problem of the slavery past. But I find it equally difficult to know what to suggest as appropriate public acts of recognition of that past and the need to provide a measure of recompense. My bewilderment or loss is as true for Britain as for other European countries such as France, the Netherlands, Denmark, Spain, Portugal and so forth – all of whom at one point or another were active participants in what a recent BBC drama series entitled *A Respectable Trade* (the story is set in Bristol but could equally have been set in Bordeaux, Amsterdam or a number of other European cities). If I were pushed, however, to make a suggestion as a possible way forward, my ideas would be along the following lines.

First, there needs to be a recognition of the achievements of Africans in the Atlantic world. With little or nothing, ex-slaves and their descendants have constructed societies that could serve as models (not without significant imperfections) that could be emulated by communities beset by conflict bred of ethnic and racial diversity. Second, whilst it is now too late to sensibly distribute starting-up funds to African communities in the West and make land available, there may still be space and time for financial and commercial enterprises, universities and other major institutions as well as for families and corporate bodies who benefited directly or indirectly form slavery, to take positive steps to encourage active African participation in the total life of societies on the Atlantic rim. This can be done through favourable loans, training, scholarships and so forth for the present generation of African descendants in the West.

The difficulty here is that such schemes would have to recognize and act upon the need to empower individuals who exhibit the potential for growth. This would be neither 'positive discrimination' nor preferential treatment. Africans in the Atlantic world are great believers in the virtues of individuality, and would want to compete with others for potentially rewarding positions in government, business, the professions and so forth. But for a period of fifty years or so, beginning sometime in the early years of the next century, banks and other financial institutions, schools and universities, government departments and related bodies, churches and other major institutions (such as museums) could establish funds and opportunities specifically targeting candidates from African communities who wish to avail themselves of these facilities.

There would also be a need for such efforts to have at least the following controlling characteristics. In the first place a national dimension is required. Specific nation states in Europe and the Americas would be expected to exhibit specific plans about how they would set about contributing to this effort. Second, this endeavour would be larger than the Marshall Plan for the recovery of Germany and Japan after the Second World War, but would learn from that historic effort. Third, international bodies (such as the World Bank, the IMF and the UN) and various regional bodies would play major roles. Fourth, non-governmental organizations, charitable organizations, museums, academic bodies would be integrated into whatever initiative were discussed and taken up by specific bodies or nation states. Finally, this Marshall Plan-like effort would eschew any central role by corrupt, non-democratic governments in Africa, the Caribbean or the United States of America.

Initially, these efforts will be plagued by right-wing commentators making the point that some people are not being treated fairly whilst other people are not worthy of what they receive from society. Therefore the initiative would need to be accompanied by an educational effort, putting before the wider public the historical facts about the injustice of slavery and explaining how this continues into the present; the public must be made to know that accumulation of wealth by individuals, families and communities in the past was only possible on the basis of protection from one authority or the other, nearly always the state and the overarching ideology that based rights to possession and success on colour, not necessarily ability. Second, individuals must compete for what they receive, so as to uphold the fundamental democratic principle of equality of opportunity through merit and ability.

In short, I do not think that there can be only one or two types of commemoration or of efforts to compensate for slavery. It will always be a deep scar, a blot on the record of Western or European civilization, with which Europeans as well as the African diaspora will have to live. The moral message from that past lives with us: mankind's inhumanity to itself for profit must be taboo; just as injustice and discrimination on the basis of race, ethnicity, colour, etc., must be taboo; the rigours of the law must uphold such principles. Monuments to humanity's failure in this regard must be woven into the mainstream of major European societies such as Britain and the Netherlands, but it must be left to governmental as well as civic groups to determine how best this can be done. Museums, statues, incorporation of slavery in the Americas into European school books, are all ways in which several small things can be done. I wager that a multitude of such small things will amount to more than just one or two big statues or exhibitions.

I have deliberately set aside any consideration of the situation in Africa. This is because African societies – particularly their chiefs – were themselves involved as active partners in the trade, albeit in a situation of unequal exchange. Additionally, the trade involved piracy and conquest and deliberate exploitation of the weaker by the stronger. Nonetheless, some African societies must bear some responsibility for the trade, and whilst there is a need to address or redress the centuries-old unequal exchange between Africa and Europe and America, this can be handled by Western states, particularly Britain, France and Belgium, establishing, perhaps through the Lomé Conventions, more favourable terms of trade, systems of control for unproductive corruption and ending the highly unfavourable burden of debt set out in the arrangements for political independence in such places as Kenya and Zimbabwe, where Africans have had to pay Europeans for lands stolen and continue to pay for the debts incurred by brutal governments established and run for the exclusive good of European settlers.

There are, of course, several cans of worms to be opened as we have just entered a new millennium. This may be an unpleasant experience, but they should nonetheless be opened to the light of day.

James Walvin

## Slavery, Truth and Reconciliation

In these days of 'truth and reconcilation', a large number of nations have begun to come to terms with the sins and wrongdoings of their past. Most recently the South African Truth and Reconcilation Commission has sought to begin healing historical and contemporary wounds by truth-telling and by public exposure of recent crimes and misdemeanours. But South Africa is only the latest in a range of countries attempting to come to terms with a tortured past, by boldly confronting painful realities. Since 1945 the long list is growing by the year. The crimes of Nazi Germany, the former communist regimes and ex-dictatorships worldwide have been forced to confront the wrongdoings of the recent past. The settling of old scores has taken a number of forms, from brutal show trials and executions (Ceausescu), through elaborately-orchestrated legal scrutiny (Nuremburg), to a wave of contemporary chest-beating (Australian Aboriginal rights).

The more we consider national crimes, the clearer it becomes that such problems have deep historical roots whose consequences continue to bedevil modern western societies. This is perhaps nowhere more apparent than in the matter of colonial and imperial history.

The consequences of European expansion, trade and settlement globally, rarely favoured native peoples. The collapse of the Amerindian civilizations of Central and South America (the Aztec, Maya and Inca), the decimation of Amerindian peoples throughout the hemisphere, the horrible fate of Aboriginal peoples in Australia: the list goes on and on. Yet there is one particular consequence of this European colonial past which has a distinctive and continuing resonance through to the present day: Atlantic slavery.

The enormity of the Atlantic slave trade is beyond all doubt. Approximately twelve million Africans were loaded onto European (and American) slave ships for the pestilential oceanic crossing to the Americas. About ten and a half million survived this journey. About seven per cent were destined for what became the United States of America; the largest numbers went to the West Indies and Brazil. In the first instance the great majority of all Africans transported were destined for the sugar fields. It is a curiosity: millions of Africans shipped into the Americas by Europeans, to produce luxurious tropical commodities (sugar, rum, tobacco, rice) which Europeans had managed perfectly well without previously. In the process, the Europeans enhanced their material and commercial well-being (examples can be found in the history of Bristol, Liverpool, Nantes and Bordeaux), secured important beachheads in the Americas and the Caribbean, and helped pave the way towards the subsequent European invasions and settlement of the interior of America. Without the African, this would have been impossible. Some simple figures provide further clues. Before 1820, approximately two and a half million Europeans had crossed the Atlantic to settle in the Americas. But in the same period, more than *eight million* Africans had been shipped across the Atlantic. Who, then, were the real pioneers of settlement in the Americas? Before 1800, something like eighty per cent of all the women and ninety per cent of all the children who had moved across the Atlantic were African.[1]

This trade in humanity had untold and generally dire consequences for Africa itself. From Senegambia to Angola and onto Mozambique, and from ever-deeper into the continent's interior, Africans of hugely-varying cultures, were brutally enslaved and passed on to Europeans for oceanic transportation. Few now doubt that it formed a bleak and violent theme in more than four centuries of African history. These African slaves served to shape the course of history in the Americas. Their muscle power and skills brought profitable cultivation to wild but fertile regions. Africans and Europeans, however, have also had a dire impact on the Amerindian peoples. Finally, Atlantic slavery greatly benefited the people who had orchestrated this infernal system: Europeans, who were living securely in their maritime metropoles. The rise of western material wealth – still clearly visible for all in Amsterdam and London – cannot be disentangled from the fruits of slave labour in the Americas.

Historians have long been aware of this extraordinary story, but in recent years it has spilled out from the confines of academe to find a niche in the public memory. Sections of that same public are now anxious to seek redress/explanation/truth-telling about this brutal aspect of Europe's recent history. It was once easy to forget what Europeans had brought about in Africa and the Americas, mainly because these events unfolded on the far side of the Atlantic; they were out-of-sight and therefore out-of-mind. Recent years, however, have seen a major shift in public perception.

Firstly, a new generation of European-born black people, children of West Indians who had migrated to Europe on the wave of postcolonial, post-1945 migrations, have come to demand a different kind of history: a history which pays proper regard to formerly oppressed peoples and to the relationship between European colonialism and Africa. Secondly, former colonial peoples,

---

[1] Figures taken from conference on the Slave Trade, Williamsburg, September 1998.

in Africa, Asia and the Americas, have themselves begun to rewrite their own history, casting aside metropolitan-based, Eurocentric approaches and values which (inevitably) shaped earlier historical interpretations. This process has been driven forward by the dramatic changes in the social experience *within the* United States. Especially since the mid-1950s, the rise of black consciousness in the United States, voter registration and the insistence on full civil rights have helped to transform the history of slavery and its consequences in North America. The changing historiography of North America has also served to push historians of other regions into new, innovative approaches.

We can now appreciate that blacks have a history in Europe which long predates the post-1945 migrations. Britain (especially London) had a black population of between five and ten thousand in 1800. Parish registers, family portraits, legal cases – all and more tell the story of British black history. The emergent awareness of this history has helped transform the wider story of British (and European) history, and has compounded demands that Britain – like other slave trading nations – comes to terms with the consequences of its historical deeds.

In Britain these consequences have been remarkable, notwithstanding the continuing difficulty of persuading people of the centrality of slavery in recent British (and European) history. Ironically, the British role in abolition has not helped. The British abolition of slave trade (1807) and slavery (1834-1838) has in fact helped to distort British historical perceptions. The emphasis on the high-minded British virtue behind abolition has created an historical amnesia towards the British role in Atlantic slavery itself. It is important not to forget that in the years *before* abolition, in the years when the British began to sing 'Rule Britannia' (with its ironic lines 'Britons never, ever shall be slaves'), the British shipped something like three million Africans into American bondage. After 1807, however, the world's leading slave trader became the loudest and most assertive abolitionist. It was a stunning role reversal, still in need of full historical explanation. There has, as a result, been a British tendency to bask in the story of abolition – forgetting the British involvement in slavery.

The Public Memory

The public has become increasingly aware of slavery. Films (*Amistad*) novels (*Beloved*), television series (*Roots*) have confirmed and hastened the process. So too has the recent demand for reparations (based on the Israel/Germany model) for slavery, promoted by the Organisation of African Unity based in Nairobi. In Britain these demands have been adopted by prominent spokesmen of the local black community. Demands for a reappraisal of Britain's past have been driven forward by a number of important events and innovations. The decision to establish a permanent slave trade exhibition at the Maritime Museum in Liverpool in 1996 was a major breakthrough. But it was secured against a host of problems and objections from local pressure groups. In the event, the exhibit has proved hugely successful, attracting large numbers of appreciative visitors. It now seems the obvious thing to do – to commemorate the slave trade in the city which dispatched one half of all British slave ships.

There have been other important commemorations. In 1996 the *Equiano Society* (named after Britain's most famous eighteenth-century black resident) was formed to celebrate the contribution of people of West Indian origin to the development of British life. In 1997 the National Portrait Gallery in London held a major exhibit devoted to black history in Britain. The exhibition was centred around the life and times of Ignatius Sancho, the ex-slave and man of letters who died in London in 1780. In 1998 major television networks celebrated the fiftieth anniversary of the 1948 arrival of West Indians, and their subsequent impact on British life. Indeed this impact is now so obvious and celebrated widely; from the number of black sportsmen who play soccer and cricket for England, through to the iconography of the black past which is extensively used in posters, adverts and the like.

Historians involved in these events sometimes found the process difficult, not least because of the *nature* of the subsequent debates. The issues at stake are not merely academic, but have a powerful contemporary and social resonance. It is no easy matter to unite black and white, left and right, on the propriety or the nature of historical reconstruction. In the event, these major exhibitions proved hugely successful – and a vindication of the initial decision to launch the schemes.

This is not, however, a static process (the opening of this or that exhibition). It is important to keep the process moving – not least by professionals in the field. There is no *single* way of commemorating the historical relationship between Europe and slavery. Historians, the professionals who *bear witness* to the truth, need to lend their expertise to others anxious to promote an historical reappraisal which makes sense for a broader public.

My own suggestions for memorializing slavery in other countries, are of course based on my experiences of involvement in a similar process in Britain. I was guest curator at Liverpool. It is important to have a broad point of view, and not to concentrate on a *single* event or institution. It is best to proceed with a small group of informed and committed people (though this group will need to expand with time to incorporate key areas of non-academic life – without becoming too large). Think for example of maritime and commercial issues; where can slavery be best remembered in an *institutional* location? Think of a major exhibition which is permanent – or which travels. Liverpool's exhibition may soon be 'cloned' in New York. Think of television and radio programmes; of publications which reach beyond academe. Think of ways of remembering the impact of slavery on metropolitan cultures (broadly defined). More than that, here is an opportunity for historians to make a critical (and immediate) impact in a field which is of contemporary importance. It will not be without its difficulties. But it is certainly pressing and worthwhile.

Ratan Vaswani

## A Respectable Trade

Kidnapping, forced exile, mutilation, rape, torture and imprisonment. The whole nauseating business of slavery helped finance some of Bristol's finest Georgian architecture. Yet only at the start of the twenty-first century did the city finally open, in one of its many first-class museums, a permanent exhibition about what men of refinement once called 'the respectable trade'.

Bristol and Transatlantic Slavery opened at Bristol Industrial Museum in April 2000. Sue Giles, curator of ethnography and foreign archaeology at Bristol City Museum and Art Gallery, oversaw the transfer of the 1999 temporary exhibition on which the new display was based from her museum to its present, dockside home. She believes that it is an important addition to the museum's displays. 'This is a multicultural city. All parts of the population have a right to see their story represented', she says. 'But this isn't about so-called political correctness. Visitors, black and white, said they wanted the temporary exhibition to be made permanent. Slavery was a piece of the historical jigsaw missing from the rest of Bristol's story exhibited in the city. We needed both to complete and set the record straight so that rumours and myths aren't forever perpetuated.'

The success of the temporary exhibition – 160,000 visitors in six months – was in no small measure due to ongoing collaboration with members of the African Caribbean community, which, at six per cent of the city's population, is the largest of Bristol's diverse ethnic groups. Christine Jackson, outreach and programming manager at Bristol City Museum and Art Gallery, set up consultative groups. Their recommendations informed an initial leaflet addressing stories of slavery, connections with certain sites and a small, permanent display at the Georgian House Museum about its residents, including a slave, Pero, who now has a bridge named after him.

Jackson and Giles concur in their belief that the partnership 'has been a voyage of discovery as much for the museum service as for all the people who came forward with proposals, beginning at the Malcolm X Centre in St Pauls' – where many of Bristol's African Caribbean residents live. The community thought there were hoards of material related to slavery in the city that were kept hidden. Museum officers were worried there wasn't enough: 'We did some lateral thinking about our collections which stimulated us to think again about material like portraits of sugar merchants', says Christine Jackson. Slave trade initiatives also generated poetry, Bristol schoolchildren exchanged art with counterparts in Ghana, and African music was explored in an exhibition that featured live drumming.

The reactions to the 1999 Bristol show compared well with the hostility expressed in some quarters towards the National Maritime Museum's Wolfson Gallery of Trade and Empire, which also opened in 1999. The Greenwich displays were slated on the letters page of *The Daily Telegraph* and accused of distorting history, not just by conservatives but also by more liberal voices.

An exhibit featuring a mannequin of an upper-crust eighteenth-century woman drinking tea aroused particular controversy and was eventually withdrawn. The trades in tea, the sugar that sweetened it and slaves were intertwined, the caption declared. But for many this piece proved hard to fathom. In October 1999 the museum held a conference, 'Exhibiting Empires', which explored representations of British imperialism. Some delegates expressed confusion as to what questions were being raised and what the answers might be. Were we to understand that the horrors of slavery were the product of complex market forces? Did tea drinkers, or even, specifically, lady tea drinkers deserve a particular share of blame? Were those who preferred one lump, not two, only half as guilty?

A responsible history of slavery, or more generally, of imperialism, cannot help but raise the issue of how to treat the wounds of racism. But at Trade and Empire the designers had depersonalized the non-white presence. Visitors met the gaze of the elegant white lady tea drinker, complete in every detail, as one individual to another. The part played by slaves in the refined pastime of tea drinking was, by contrast, represented by a manacled black hand rising from a cargo hatch. An attempt to show how white capitalism denied the humanity of its black victims? Two teenage girls I observed, catching sight of the hand as they walked past, began to giggle. What was needed here and in other parts of the gallery dealing with slavery, was an attempt to engage with

'The Price of Tea', the controversial tableau at the National Maritime Museum, Greenwich. The exhibit was eventually withdrawn. © National Maritime Museum, London.

the stories of real people, with names and faces, who, although they ended up as chattel, were born free. There was little recognition of pre-enslavement identities as family members, craftspeople, musicians... people who led meaningful lives in the rich culture of West Africa.

Standards for the representation of slavery in British museums have not been set by the National Maritime Museum but by those in Bristol and Liverpool. The Merseyside Maritime Museum first put slavery on the museum agenda in 1994 and has been forthright in aiming for emotional impact, intellectual rigour and sensitivity as it tries to redress neglect of black history. The Transatlantic Slavery exhibition follows four fictive Africans, with names and faces, from life in Africa through the Middle Passage and on to the New World. Visitors are presented with punishment collars and shackles and pass through a darkened cargo hull on to which are projected sinister, flickering images of life below decks. On exit from the gallery there are moving video testimonies from British descendants of slaves. Leaving the Bristol displays visitors are given the opportunity to respond emotionally on a comments board. Before eventually following suit and introducing a 'democracy wall', there was, on exit from Trade and Empire, minimally interpreted footage from Carry on up the Khyber, a 1960s British film comedy dependent for laughs on racist caricature.

Achieving balance in their treatment of slavery has been difficult for all three cities. In Liverpool they succeeded but had a harder job winning over a much bigger, more politicized African Caribbean community than in Bristol.

Despite accusations of misrepresenting those who worked for the abolition of slavery, the National Maritime Museum has not, in the process of reassessing empire from a postcolonial perspective, forced honourable players in the story to walk the plank. Trade and Empire

'The Crossing', at the National Maritime Museum, Greenwich.
© National Maritime Museum, London.

accurately points out that, while imperial British merchant shipping had much to answer for in perpetuating the slave trade, the Royal Navy played a significant part in its abolition. Indeed the message was reiterated by replacing the controversial tea-party exhibit with a ship's figurehead showing George IV as a benign Roman emperor, surrounded by freed slaves.

Both in society and in museums, there should be a commitment to determine what really happened, so that racial healing, still far from complete, can progress. Therefore, standard accounts of slavery may also have to be questioned by investigating one other, crucial, matter. To what extent was the overseas transport of Africans by Europeans dependent on the prior overland transport of Africans by Africans? Trade and Empire shies away from that question. In the light of some excellent television documentaries in recent years, it is, however, a painful but important one for postcolonial people living together, often in mixed-race families.

Peter Bowen's father is mixed-race Guyanese, his mother white English. He teaches history at a school in North Westminster, which may be one of the most culturally diverse communities in the country. 'My students', he says, when discussing museums and colonialism, 'are eager to learn how people of colour got here and want information about perpetrators and victims. They understand subtleties. I also want to probe more deeply with them questions of identity, origins and destinies. I have yet to go on a museum visit where any real answers emerge.'

Bowen hasn't been to Bristol, where chilling contemporary testimonies played over headphones concede, such as those of Ottobah Cuguano in 1787, that Africans kept and traded in slaves. The exhibition points out, however, that it was Europeans who introduced chattel slavery to Africa and that 'though both Africans and Europeans participated in the transatlantic slave trade, it was

A Young Visitor traces the journey at the Merseyside Maritime Museum. Credit: The Board of Trustees of National Museums and Galleries on Merseyside. © National Maritime Museum, London.

European demand which drove it and Europe which benefited'. No more, no less, than the facts. In all the consultations undertaken by the team at Bristol, this was what people said they wanted and expected from the museum service. Both local visitors and visitors from Africa, including the Gambian High Commissioner, have praised Bristol Museum for its presentations.

Bristol's black community also stressed that it wanted its struggle represented. A striking image in the new permanent display is that of the 'logo' of the British Abolition movement. A kneeling slave asks for aid from his (and her) white brethren. The text points out that the passive role of the African belies the truth of the fight against slavery. Through open rebellion, subversion and sabotage, slaves themselves helped defeat slavery by making it economically unviable. The closing 'Legacies' section of the exhibition brings the story up to date. In the temporary exhibition there was a 1963 photograph of people discussing tactics during the Bristol Bus Boycott, the first black-led campaign in Britain against racism in employment.

The National Maritime Museum's publicity promises that the 'colonization in reverse' of Deptford by black sailors from the eighteenth century onwards will be one of the 'hidden and forgotten histories' it draws out. Tantalizingly, it is left undeveloped. It's a real pity. Trade and Empire is at its best when it gets closest to home. It manages, for example, through The Crossing, an installation commissioned from carnival costume makers, to celebrate, in a refreshingly uncliched way, West London's Notting Hill Carnival and the vibrancy of British African Caribbean culture generally.

The museum could have got even closer and dealt with a matter of national significance that took place in south east London. This would have given Trade and Empire the harder, sobering punch that is packed at the exhibitions in Merseyside and Bristol. In Eltham, a few miles down

'Sold down the River' by Tony Forbes, the Artist's view of what it means to be young and black in a city with a slaving past. © Tony Forbes.

the road from the National Maritime Museum in Greenwich, the family of Stephen Lawrence have waged a high profile campaign for Britain to face up to the consequences of racism and its roots in slavery and colonialism. It doesn't get a mention. The original Bristol displays included a photograph of Marlon Thomas, left for dead after a racist attack on Durdham Down in 1994. To date Thomas has received no compensation.

Although not stemming directly from the recommendations of the MacPherson Report into the Lawrence murder, Bristol museums have shown a commitment to attitude training. On hearing through the grapevine that front-of-house staff thought 'trouble' would be arriving on their doorstep during the 1999 exhibition in Bristol, two training sessions were held, without managers present, led by community activist Mikey Dread and Paul Courtier, director of Bristol Race Equality Council. The exhibition and staff concerns relating to it were discussed. There has been no trouble. The front-of-house staff are committed to the new permanent exhibition, as part of the ongoing transformation of Bristol Industrial Museum into a future Museum of Bristol which will house a more complete, permanent social history of the city. It deserves every success.

A spirit husband from Baule, Ivory Coast, an object used to illustrate pre-enslavement identity and culture at the Bristol Industrial Museum. © 'Bristol Museums and Art Gallery'.

The Contributors

Ama Ata Aidoo (Ghana, 1940)
is a writer, Professor of Literature and consultant on education and gender issues. She graduated from the University of Ghana, was a fellow of the Advanced Creative Writing Program at Stanford University (Palo Alto, USA) and in the early 1980s, a Minister of Education (Ghana). Currently, she is a columnist for *The New Internationalist Magazine*, and Project Initiator and Executive Director of Mbaasem ('women's words, women's affairs'), a foundation to establish and maintain a writers' retreat. From late March 2001, she is in Sweden as the first Guest Author at the Nordic African Institute of the University of Uppsala, Uppsala. Her books include *Changes* (1991), for which she received the Commonwealth Writers' Prize for Africa in 1992, *Someone Talking to Sometime* (1986) winner of the Nelson Mandela Prize for Poetry in 1987, *The girl Who Can and Other Stories* (1997), *The Dilemma of a Ghost* (1960) and *Anowa* (1970) drama, and many other works.

Hilary McD. Beckles (Barbados, 1955)
is Professor of Economic and Social History at the University of the West Indies in Kingston, Jamaica. His books include *White Servitude and Black Slavery in Barbados 1627-1715* (1989), *Natural Rebels: A Social History of Enslaved Black Women in Barbados 1680-1838* (1989) and *Gendering Women in Caribbean Slave Society* (1999).

Allison Blakely (Alabama, U.S.A., 1940),
is Professor of European and Comparative History at Howard University in Washington, D.C. He earned his Ph.D. in Modern European History at the University of California in Berkeley in 1971. He has published various studies on European dimensions of the African Diaspora, including *Russia and the Negro: Blacks in Russian History and Thought* (1986) and *Blacks in the Dutch World: The Evolution of Racial Imagery in a Modern Society* (1994). He is currently working on a more comprehensive history of Blacks in modern Europe. In the Fall of 2001, he will join Boston University as a Professor of History and African-American Studies.

Ina Césaire (Martinique)
is a writer, ethnologist and maker of film documentaries. Her play *Trafic triangulaire* (Triangular trade) was presented in Fort-de-France on May 22, 1998 as a remembrance of the slave revolt.

Seymour Drescher (New York, U.S.A., 1934)
is University Professor of History and Professor of Sociology at the University of Pittsburgh. His most recent publications include *From Slavery to Freedom: Comparative Studies in the Rise and Fall of Atlantic Slavery* (1999), *A Historical Guide to World Slavery* (co-editor, 1998) and *Slavery* (co-editor, 2001). He is also the author of *Econocide: British Slavery in the Era of Abolition* (1977), *Capitalism and Antislavery: British Mobilization in Comparative Perspective* (1986) and a contributor to *Fifty Years Later: Antislavery, Capitalism and Modernity,* ed. Gert Oostindie (1995/1996) and to *The Jews and the Expansion of Europe to the West, 1450-1800,* eds Paolo Bernardini and Norman Fiering (2001).

Lowell Fiet (Wisconsin, U.S.A., 1948)
teaches Caribbean literature at the University of Puerto Rico at Río Piedras. A playwright and theatre critic, initially for the *San Juan Star*, now for *Claridad*, he edits the journal *Sargasso*, directs the Tdlmag theatre collective, heads the Caribbean 2000 Reasearch Project in Humanities at his university, and publishes studies on comparative Caribbean theatre and performance. His edited books include *Caribe 2000: Definiciones, identidades y culturas regionales y/o nacionales* (1997), *Caribe 2000: Hablar, nombrar, pertenecer* (1998), *A Gathering of Players and Poets* (1999), and *Sargasso: Performance and Text in Caribbean Literature and Art* (2000).

Flávio dos Santos Gomes (Brazil, 1964)
is Associate Professor of History at the Federal University of Rio de Janeiro. His M.A. dissertation, entitled *Histórias de Quilombolas. Mocambos e comunidades de senzalas no Rio de Janeiro, século XIX,* was awarded the Arquivo Nacional Award (1993), and was published in 1995. His research is focused on marronage, revolt and slave resistance, kinship, black family and peasantry among

slave communities in different Brazilian regions. His publications include the edited volume *Nas Terras do Cabo Norte. Fronteiras, Colonização e Escravidão na Guiana Brasileira – Séculos XVIII-XIX* (1999), and a study on slave, runaway, peasant, and Amerindian communities in Northern Brazil, *Hydra e os Pântanos. Mocambos e Quilombos no Brasil Escravista – Séculos XVII-XIX* (2001).

Harry Goulbourne (Jamaica, 1948)
is Professor of Sociology and Director of the Race and Ethnicity Research Unit, of South Bank University, London. His teaching career includes Senior Lectureships at the universities of Dar-es-Salaam, Tanzania, the University of the West Indies, Jamaica, and the University of Warwick. His publications and (co-)edited books include *Caribbean Families in the Trans-Atlantic World* (2000), *Race Relations in Britain since 1945* (1998); *Ethnicity and Nationalism in Post-Imperial Britain* (1991), *Democracy and Socialism in Africa* (1991), and *Black Politics in Britain* (1990).

Ruben Gowricharn (Suriname, 1952)
studied non-Western Sociology at Leiden University, and continued to live in the Netherlands since. He published widely on Suriname and on minorities and ethnicity in the Netherlands. His recent books include *Hollandse contrasten. Over de keerzijde van sociale integratie* (1998) and *Andere gedachten. Over de multiculturele samenleving* (2000). At the moment he is editing a special issue of the *Journal of International Migration and Integration* (2001) on minority elites in western countries. Gowricharn is Senior Researcher at the University of Amsterdam.

Frank Martinus Arion (Curaçao, 1936)
is writer and director of the Instituto Lingwistiko Antiano in Curaçao. He defended a thesis on the origins of Papiamentu (*The Kiss of a Slave*, 1996) at the University of Amsterdam. He published the novels *Dubbelspel* (1973), *Afscheid van de koningin* (1975), *Nobele wilden* (1979), and *De laatste vrijheid* (1995).

Achille Mbembe (Cameroon)
is a historian and currently a Senior Research Fellow at the Institute for Social and Economic Research at the University of the Witwatersrand, Johannesburg, South Africa. He was Professor of History at Columbia University (New York City, USA) and the University of Pennsylvania (Philadelphia, USA) before becoming the Executive Secretary of the Council for the Development of Social Science Research in Africa (CODESRIA). This Council was granted a Prince Claus Award in 1997. Achille Mbembe is the author of, among many other books, *On the Postcolony* (2001).

Carl Niehaus (South Africa, 1959)
was condemned in 1983 to fifteen years in prison because of his fight against the apartheid regime in his native country and his membership of the African National Congress. He was released after serving half this term, and subsequently became information officer for the ANC. In 1994 he was elected member of parliament for the ANC. From 1997 through 2000, he served as South African Ambassador to the Netherlands. He published on religion, communication and prisons, and an autobiography, *Om te veg vir hoop* (1993).

Olu Oguibe (Nigeria)
is a senior fellow of the Vera List Center for Art and Politics in New York, and author of several books, including *Uzo Egonu: An African Artist in the West*, and *Reading the Contemporary: African Art from Theory to the Marketplace*.

Gert Oostindie (the Netherlands, 1955)
is Director of the KITLV/Royal Institute of Linguistics and Anthropology in Leiden and holds a chair as Professor of Caribbean Studies at Utrecht University. His recent publications include *Knellende Koninkrijksbanden. Het Nederlandse dekolonisatiebeleid in de Caraïben, 1940-2000* (2001; 3 volumes, with Inge Klinkers), *Het verleden onder ogen. Herdenking van de slavernij* (ed., 1999), *Dromen en littekens. Dertig jaar na de Curaçaose revolte, 30 mei 1969* (ed., 1999), *Het paradijs overzee. De 'Nederlandse' Caraïben en*

*Nederland* (1997), *Ethnicity in the Caribbean* (ed., 1996), and *Fifty Years Later. Antislavery, Capitalism and Modernity in the Dutch World* (ed., 1995).

Pedro Pérez Sarduy (Cuba, 1943)
is a poet, author, and radio maker, presently living in Londen. He published among other works *Surrealidad* (1967) and *Cumbite and Other Poems* (1987, 1990). He is co-editor with Jean Stubbs of *Afro-Cuban Voices: On Race and Identity in Contemporary Cuba* (2000), and *Afro-Cuba: una antología de escritos cubanos sobre raza, política y cultura* (1993). He has finished an unpublished work, 'Journal in Babylon', a series of chronicles on Britain, and will soon publish his first novel, *Las criadas de La Habana*, based on his mother's life stories about pre-revolutionary Havana.

Richard Price (New York, U.S.A. 1941)
has been writing about the Afro-Caribbean past for four decades. Among his many books are *First-Time: The Historical Vision of an Afro-American People* (1983), *Alabi's World* (1990), and *The Convict and the Colonel* (1998). With Sally Price he has written *Two Evenings in Saramaka* (1991), *Stedman's Surinam: Life in an Eighteenth-Century Slave Society* (1992), *Equatoria* (1992), *Enigma Variations* (1995), and *Maroon Arts: Cultural Vitality in the African Diaspora* (1999). He divides his time between rural Martinique and the College of William & Mary in Virginia, where he is Duane A. and Virginia S. Dittman Professor of American Studies, Anthropology, and History.

Livio Sansone (Italy, 1956)
obtained his PhD in Anthropology at the University of Amsterdam and since 1996 has been Academic Vice-Director of the Center for Afro-Asian Studies of the Candido Mendes University in Rio de Janeiro. Starting from February 1998 he is also lecturing at the State University of Rio de Janeiro. He has published widely on race relations and black cultures in Great Britain, the Netherlands, Suriname and Brazil. His present research is on race relations and Afro-Brazilians in the Military Police of the State of Rio de Janeiro. In 2001, he will publish *Blackness Withouth Ethnicity. The Local and the Global in Brazilian Race Relations and Black Cultural Production*.

Abdul Sheriff (Zanzibar, 1939)
studied Geography and African history at the University of California at Los Angeles, and at the School of Oriental & African Studies, University of London. He joined the University of Dar es Salaam in 1969 until 1993, when he moved to Zanzibar as Advisor and Principal Curator of the Zanzibar Museums. Sheriff wrote and edited several books and many scholarly articles, including *Slaves, Spices and Ivory in Zanzibar* (1987), *Zanzibar Under Colonial Rule* (1991), *History & Conservation of Zanzibar Stone Town* (1995) and *Zanzibar Stone Town: An Architectural Exploration* (1998).

Alex van Stipriaan (the Netherlands, 1954)
is Professor of Non-Western History at the Erasmus University Rotterdam. Among his publications are *Surinaams contrast; roofbouw en overleven in een Caraïbische plantage-kolonie, 1750-1863* (1993) and a number of articles on the Afro-Surinamese history of music and dance, naming systems, marronage, religion, education, and processes of creolization. He is also a member of the board of the National Platform Dutch Slavery Past, which strives for a national monument-cum-institute.

Ratan Vaswani (Nigeria, 1961)
was educated in England and has worked in schools, colleges and universities in several countries. In 1998 he graduated with a Master's degree in Gallery Studies from the University of Essex and has been Ethics Adviser at the UK Museums Association since 1999. He leads seminars for museum professionals on ethical issues and is a regular contributor to the British *Museums Journal*. Based in London, Vaswani also teaches English as a Second Language to asylum seekers and refugees.

James Walvin (U.K., 1942)
is Professor of History at the University of York and was guest curator of the Liverpool Maritime Museum for the Atlantic Slave Trade exhibition. He published many books on slavery and modern social history, including *An African's Life. The Life and Time of Olaudah Equiano* (1998), *Fruits of Empire* (1997), and *Black Ivory* (1996).

Nigel Worden (U.K., 1955)
is Professor of History at the University of Cape Town. His research focuses on the history of slavery at the Cape, the roots of the Cape slave trade in South and South-East Asia, and Cape Town in the Dutch East India Company period. His publications include *Slavery in Dutch South Africa* (1985), *The making of modern South Africa* (1994) and *Cape Town: The Making of a City* (1998). He has also published in the field of public history and heritage studies in South Africa.

I should express my heartfelt thanks to the Prince Claus Fund, for stimulating and financing first the Dutch edition, *Het verleden onder ogen* (1999), and next this substantially revised English edition. More particularly, I owe gratitude to the Fund's director Els van der Plas and to Geerte Wachter, for their enthusiasm and support for the whole project since 1999, as well as, for the present edition, to Carla Wauman. Finally, I thank the translators for splendid jobs; Inge Klinkers for her careful and cheerful editorial assistance; Irma Boom and Sanne Beeren for the imaginative book design.